D1369988

The Four
Imperatives
of a
Successful School

In loving memory of my father, George Edward Gillespie, who was such a strong supporter of me and of my work.

The Four Imperatives of a Successful School

Lynn G. Beck
Joseph Murphy

CORWIN PRESS, INC.
A Sage Publications Company
Thousand Oaks, California

For information address:

Corwin Press, Inc.
A Sage Publications Company
2455 Teller Road
Thousand Oaks, California 91320
E-mail: order@corwin.sagepub.com

SAGE Publications Ltd.
6 Bonhill Street
London EC2A 4PU
United Kingdom

SAGE Publications India Pvt. Ltd.
M-32 Market
Greater Kailash I
New Delhi 110 048 India

3-13-97

Printed in the United States of America

Library of Congress Cataloging-in-Publication Data

Beck, Lynn G.
    The four imperatives of a successful school /
Lynn G. Beck, Joseph Murphy.
        p. cm.
    Includes bibliographical references (p.) and index.
    ISBN 0-8039-6279-7 (Cloth: acid-free paper).—ISBN 0-8039-6280-0
(pbk.: acid-free paper)
    1. School-based management—California—Los Angeles—
Case studies. 2. School management and organization—California—
Los Angeles—Case studies. 3. Educational change—California—
Los Angeles—Case studies. I. Murphy, Joseph, 1949- . II. Title.
LB2806.35.B43 1996
371.2′009794′94—dc20   96-10089

This book is printed on acid-free paper.

96 97 98 99 10 9 8 7 6 5 4 3 2 1

Corwin Press Production Editor: Diana E. Axelsen
Typesetter: Marion S. Warren

Contents

Introduction

Analysts of educational reform are quick to point out that efforts to centralize school governance and attempts to move authority to local sites often appear as alternating patterns in reform plans and proposals (e.g., Elmore, 1993; Hanson, 1991; Malen, Ogawa, & Kranz, 1989; Mirel, 1990; Tyack, 1993). Most also agree that for the past decade or so, the push for decentralization has dominated the reform scene with voices from many quarters heralding attempts to devolve power from federal, state, and district levels to principals, teachers, and parents. Underlying the calls for site-based management (SBM) of schools are a limited knowledge base and a host of assumptions about the actual and ideal governance of schools and the ways that decision-making structures influence learning and teaching.

In an earlier volume (Murphy & Beck, 1995), we considered ideas and assumptions that have undergirded and shaped current initiatives to decentralize governance to local school sites. Furthermore, we examined the evidence on the efficacy of SBM as a school reform and drew preliminary conclusions about the ways in which empirical data support or challenge the theories embedded in SBM. Ultimately, we concluded that SBM appears to be "a fairly weak intervention in our arsenal of school reform measures" (p. 178) and that we cannot detect ways that SBM, as it has been implemented, has resulted in widespread, measurable, and positive changes in learning and teaching. At the same time, however, we acknowledged limitations in our ability to draw definitive conclusions from the evidence that has been collected to date. For example, we noted that generalizing about SBM is difficult because definitions of and theories about this reform strategy are complex, motivation for decentralization is not uniform, and SBM as proposed and practiced often varies greatly across sites. Also, some researchers, seeking to test the efficacy of SBM, have been confronted with situations where site-level decision making has been only partially implemented (e.g., David, 1989; Malen et al., 1989; Rutherford, 1992; Wohlstetter & Odden, 1992). Under these conditions, scholars have been able to draw only tentative conclusions regarding SBM and educational improvement.

Cognizant of the difficulties of research on the efficacy of complex policies that are implemented with great variation, we undertook an investigation in which we shifted the focus away from evaluating SBM and toward understanding the ways SBM actually operates in a school that is successfully transforming itself. In other words, we sought to (a) identify forces that seemed to be contributing to reform in one institution operating under an SBM decision-making model; (b) untangle the various impulses and activities spurring change to see if and how governance structures interact with other factors to promote, maintain, or undermine positive movement; and (c) consider our findings in light of theoretical work on SBM with an eye to refining notions about the ways this reform strategy does or might lead to improved schools and about the conditions under which improvement might occur.

This volume contains a report of this research and is organized in the following manner. In Chapter 1, we begin with a brief review of what in our earlier volume (Murphy & Beck, 1995) we call "the logic of SBM" (p. 20). We use this phrase to refer to assumptions or hypotheses about the ways SBM contributes to good schools. In undertaking this review, we examine both conceptual analyses and empirical work on SBM and review a model that depicts "the expected effects of shared governance" (p. 11). We then discuss the study that anchors this volume and note ways in which our investigation builds on and yet differs from other work done in this area. In essence, we contend that the tremendous variation among sites attempting SBM makes empirical efforts to test hypotheses about the general effectiveness of this reform strategy by seeking to link it causally with specific outcomes an unsatisfactory endeavor. We assert that in-depth investigation into the ways SBM works within a school that is engaging in successful reform yields greater purchase for those interested in understanding this concept, for such research enables us to better understand the conditions under which schools actually change.

Chapter 2 contains a report of our investigation at Jackson Elementary School.[1] The chapter opens with a general description of the school. We then move quickly into narratives of life at Jackson, with the dual goals of portraying the actors who are shaping the transformation at this site and describing their activities, attitudes, and behaviors. Our intent is to enable readers to understand the individuals who inhabit this school; to grasp some of the structures and policies that are influencing the behaviors, commitments, and attitudes of parents, teachers, and students; and to experience, in some measure, the culture of this site.

In Chapters 3 through 6, we analyze our findings by considering four conditions contributing to the successful functioning of Jackson as an SBM school. We refer to these conditions as the four imperatives of successful schools and identify them under the broad categories of (a) a consistent and powerful focus on learning; (b) strong, yet facilitative, leadership; (c) a commitment to nurturing a sense of internal and external community; and (d) resources aimed at building the capacity of persons within the community to lead, learn, and teach.

We conclude in Chapter 7 with some thoughts about SBM and genuine school reform. We offer a set of ideas about policies, structures, and professional development that in our view are likely to enhance positive educational change and to increase the odds that SBM and other macrolevel reform strategies might have a role to play in this endeavor.

☐ **Note**

1. This is a pseudonym, as are all proper names associated with this specific site. Other details, however, such as the location of Jackson School in urban Los Angeles and its participation in a citywide school reform effort sponsored by the Los Angeles Educational Alliance for Restructuring Now (LEARN), are factual.

About the Authors

LYNN G. BECK, Ph.D., is Associate Professor of Education and Co-director of Center X, a center devoted to the preparation and development of urban school professionals, at the University of California, Los Angeles. She is the author of *Understanding the Principalship: Metaphorical Themes, 1920s-1990s* (1993, with Joseph Murphy), *Reclaiming Educational Administration as a Caring Profession* (1994), *Ethics in Educational Leadership Program: An Expanding Role* (1994, with Joseph Murphy), and *School-Based Management as School Reform: Taking Stock* (1995, with Joseph Murphy). Beck's research and teaching interests focus on the principalship, the preparation of educational leaders, and ethical dimensions of educational administration.

JOSEPH MURPHY, Ph.D., is Professor and Chair of the Department of Educational Leadership at Peabody College of Vanderbilt University. He is also Vice President of Division A of AERA and Chair of the Interstate School Leaders Licensure Consortium. His primary interest is in school improvement, with an emphasis on the role of policy. Recent volumes in this area include *School-Based Management as School Reform: Taking Stock* (1995, with Lynn G. Beck), *Restructuring Schools: Capturing and Assessing the Phenomenon*, and *The Educational Reform Movement of the 1980s: Perspectives and Cases.*

1

SBM

Mapping the Domain

The idea that authority and responsibility for curriculum, personnel, and budgets should be located within a local school site is not a new one. As Elmore (1993), Tyack (1993), and others note, despite an almost century-long "steady march" toward consolidation and bureaucratization within educational systems, the belief that control of education is best vested in local communities has persisted among many politicians, educators, and parents. Since the mid-1980s, the push for decentralization of decision making about and responsibility for schooling has been especially persistent in reform circles.

Numerous forces, it seems, have energized the decentralization movement and efforts have been made to enhance local control. For instance, in the mid-1980s, well-publicized data about the academic failures and social problems of American youth fueled efforts to reconstruct pathways of organizational and professional pathology linked to the problems identified in reform reports such as *A Nation at Risk* (National Commission on Excellence in Education, 1983), *Educating Americans for the 21st Century* (National Science Board, 1983), and *A Nation Prepared* (Carnegie Forum on Education and the Economy, 1986; Murphy, 1990). Quite often, the well-developed bureaucracies governing and controlling schools were portrayed in these reports as contributing to—if not responsible for—the failing health of American education (for discussions, see Clark & Meloy, 1989; Elmore, 1993; Murphy, 1991; Tyack, 1993). This diagnosis, supported by calls for greater involvement of teachers and parents in educational decision making (Darling-Hammond, 1988; Garms, Guthrie, & Pierce, 1978; Malen, Ogawa, & Kranz, 1989), by decentralization trends in business and industry (Mohrman, 1994; Murphy, 1991), and by antigovernment political sentiments (Murphy, 1996), promoted the adoption and implementation of various versions of local control via site-based management (SBM) within school systems across the United States (Elmore, 1993; Flax, 1989a, 1989b; Hess, 1992; Malen et al., 1989; Olson, 1991a, 1991b, 1992; Wohlstetter & Smyer, 1994).

The assortment of forces propelling SBM into the spotlight, coupled with the reality that it takes a myriad of different forms in policies and practices, makes SBM "empirically and conceptually elusive (Malen et al., 1989) and somewhat abstract" (Murphy, 1995, pp. 12-13). However, as we noted earlier, "definitions are beginning to pile up" (Murphy & Beck, 1995, pp. 12-13), and it is possible to glean from these definitions both the key elements of SBM and the central assumptions about its operation and effectiveness. In the following section, we discuss these issues. We begin with an examination of the conceptual underpinnings of SBM. Following this, we move into a brief analysis of the empirical work on this reform. In the third section of the chapter, we outline our investigation of SBM at Jackson Elementary School, noting the rationale for the study and describing our methodology.

☐ The Logic of SBM[1]

At the heart of policies advocating SBM for schools are at least six key assumptions:

1. The belief "that those most closely affected by school-level decisions—teachers, students, and parents—ought to play a significant role in making decisions" (Wohlstetter & Buffett, 1991, p. 1) about school affairs

2. The belief that "stakeholders in the school systems . . . have the right and responsibility to be involved in the decision making" (Burke, 1992, p. 38) process

3. The assumption that "students, parents, school staffs, and communities have unique needs and that these needs can best be identified and addressed by them" (Jewell & Rosen, 1993, p. 1)

4. The notion that because the school "is the fundamental decision making unit within the educational system" (Guthrie, 1986, p. 306), "schools have to [be given] the capacity to identify and respond to student needs" (Stevenson, 1990, p. 1)

5. The belief that "imposed educational decisions disempower certain categories of stakeholders" (Burke, 1992, p. 39)

6. The idea that "those actors with the best information about a particular subject should have the discretion to make decisions about that subject" (Hannaway, 1992, p. 2) and the belief that "schools often know best" (Brown, 1991, p. 3)—"the people in closest contact with students are the ones most likely to make good decisions" (Hill & Bonan, 1991, p. 6).

We contend that embedded within these assumptions is a certain logic regarding the ways in which SBM works (or should work) in schools to promote student achievement, organizational efficacy and efficiency, and satisfaction on the part of the various stakeholders affected by the educational system. Essentially, this logic assumes that this governance strategy operates as follows: SBM empowers local stakeholders; empowerment promotes ownership; ownership, in turn, increases professionalism and enhances organizational health; and, finally, changes in these two variables result in improved organizational performance.

Each of these links within the SBM chain of logic has an intuitive sense of veracity. In addition, each link draws on theory and empirical evidence for support. However, as we reveal below, both individually and collectively, the causal relationships in the SBM model are fairly weak.

□ The Evidence to Date on SBM

Prior to the mid-1980s when school site autonomy became a rallying cry for many reform efforts (Murphy, 1990), little empirical evidence existed to support the notion that this governance structure positively affected organizational or educational outcomes in schools (David, 1989; Ornstein, 1983). And the data that did exist were not glowing in their affirmation of SBM as a robust reform capable of promoting either effective participatory decision making (Conway, 1984) or "the usual goals of increased efficiency, effectiveness, or responsiveness" (Chapman & Boyd, 1986, p. 50). Interestingly, these less than positive findings, uncovered prior to the restructuring activity of the past decade, did little to deter efforts to devolve power and responsibility to lower levels in the educational hierarchy. As March and Olson (1983) conclude, even "in those rare cases where information [was] available, it [was] not attended to reliably" (p. 289). Indeed, fueled by a variety of forces and unencumbered by historical insights from previous efforts at decentralization, thinly tethered to the available research base, and armed with an unassailable belief that this time—for a variety of reasons—shared decision making would produce dramatic results, policymakers on state and district levels and administrators and teachers in local sites began to engage in efforts to move some measure of autonomy to individual school communities.

More recent efforts to study the SBM initiatives that have proliferated throughout the Western world in the past decade have resulted in a larger database on school-site autonomy. To date, however, studies have not produced strong evidence that devolving power to local communities results in better schools, more professional teachers, greater student achievement, or happier parents. Indeed, as Levine and Eubanks (1992) note in their overall assessment of SBM, "Research to date generally has reported conclusions that appear more neutral and disappointing than positive and encouraging" (p. 66). In the following passages, we review some of this evidence, using the key links in the SBM chain of logic presented above as an organizing framework.

Altered Influence Relationships

A central tenet of school-based management is that relocating influence over decisions from the state and district to the local site will enhance the power of teachers, school-level administrators, and parents. The assumption is that bureaucratic mandates, made far away from students and classrooms, inhibit the ability of educators and parents to customize curriculum and pedagogy to meet site-specific needs. If this is the case, then the logical cure would be to move responsibility for making decisions to persons possessing the most firsthand information about relevant issues. This, it is reasoned, should produce at least two benefits. First, it should enable those possessing information most relevant for the problem under consideration to participate in decision making (Galbraith, 1977; Hannaway, 1993; Mohrman, 1994). Second, devolution of power, in theory, should encourage more individuals within a local site to become involved in governance (Dellar, 1992; Malen et al., 1989; Prickett, Flangian, Richardson, & Petrie, 1990). Thus, moving authority to local sites could result in "alter[ed] influence relationships" (Malen et al., 1989, p. 10) wherein those possessing information about, and interest in, particular issues would be able to influence decisions and activities around these topics.

Evidence on the extent to which SBM actually leads to wider involvement of teachers and parents and to better decisions is decidedly mixed. Researchers report that, in some locales, site-level "councils are meeting and making important decisions" (David, 1993, p. 35) and that local "committees [have] real authority" (Goldman, Dunlap, & Conley, 1991; see also Brown, 1990; Hess, 1992; Murphy, 1994; Wohlstetter & Buffett, 1991). However, other analysts raise questions about the linkages between dispersed responsibility and genuine transformation in power structures in schools. For example, Elmore (1993) asserts that the idea of moving authority to "the school" is a vague one and that often only superficial decisions "on some limited set of dimensions" (p. 45) are released by central administrators to individual sites. Malen and her colleagues (1989) and Wohlstetter and Mohrman (1993) concur. Researchers also raise questions about the quality of the decisions made at the local site. Daresh (1992), Des Carpentrie (1995), Jenni (1990), Lindquist and Mauriel (1989), and Malen and Ogawa (1988) are among those who note that "serious decision making" (Jenni, 1990, p. 21) "over matters of importance" (Daresh, 1992, p. 115) is often not a feature of site council meetings.

Participation and Broad-Based Ownership

A second assumption about school-based management is that participants in key decisions will feel a greater sense of ownership of their school—that they will, in effect, bond more closely with their organization and feel greater enthusiasm about and commitment toward their local institutions (David, 1989). Empirical work on this proposition, again, provides a mixed picture.

On the one hand, most studies indicate that a shift to SBM in states and districts has done little to arouse greater interest in local schools on the part of the public. David (1993) and Hess (1992), for example, report that in Kentucky and Chicago, shifts to local-site autonomy had little impact on voter turnout when school related issues were on the ballot and that overall "patterns of involvement . . . [especially of] poor and minority parents" (David, 1993, p. 33) did not change with the advent of SBM.[2]

On the other hand, the evidence does suggest that greater numbers of teachers are participating in decision making under SBM. Brown (1990), Bryk (1993), Carnoy and MacDonnell (1990), Collins and Hanson (1991), Gips and Wilkes (1993), Goldman, Dunlap, and Conley (1991), and Taylor and Bogotch (1992) are among those reporting "increasing teachers' rates of participation" (Taylor & Bogotch, 1992, p. 10) in schools with some degree of local autonomy. Even this good news for advocates of SBM, however, has a downside. In particular, scholars note several problems connected with increased teacher participation in governance. For instance, Collins and Hanson (1991) and Duke, Showers, and Imber (1980) point out the high cost of participation in terms of teachers' time. Collins and Hanson (1991) further document that enthusiasm for participation peaks early in the adoption of SBM, only to drop off over time. Duke and his colleagues (1980), Malen and Ogawa (1988), and Rice and

Schneider (1992) all demonstrate that participation in many sites does not mean that teachers have substantial influence over important decisions. And Hannaway (1993), Hanson (1991), and Smith (1993) report that in some schools a small group of teachers garners most of the power and, at times, demands conformity to their ideas by exerting a fair amount of social pressure on others.

Teachers' Sense of Professionalism

Professionalism is a complex construct, one that includes numerous components, such as commitment, satisfaction, and efficacy. Although evidence from noneducational venues supports the belief that participatory management can increase the levels of each of these variables for employees, there is only spotty evidence that SBM has positively affected teacher professionalism.

Few studies, for example, have documented alterations in teachers' demonstrated commitment to their organizations. However, researchers do report that teacher-to-teacher relationships become more collegial in SBM schools (Fusarelli & Scribner, 1993). This is especially the case for those educators who participate actively in governance activities (Goldman et al., 1991; Smith, 1993).

In a similar fashion, evidence on relationships between SBM and teacher satisfaction is mixed. Some analysts (e.g., Brown, 1990; Bryk, 1993; Clune & White, 1988; Rice & Schneider, 1992; Rungeling & Glover, 1991; Steffy, 1993) have detected increases in this variable in sites where SBM is implemented in a meaningful fashion. Others (e.g., Carnoy & MacDonnell, 1990; Collins & Hanson, 1991) suggest that satisfaction rises in the early stages of implementing SBM but wanes as the innovation continues.

A sense of efficacy seems to have at least two core components. The first is the belief that one is capable of doing her or his work effectively. The second is the notion that one can make a difference in some larger sense, that an individual's work and decisions can help to bring about positive change in a system (Chapman, 1990; Murphy, Weil, Hallinger, & Mitman, 1982). A number of scholars who have examined the presence of these beliefs in SBM schools have suggested that participation in governance activities does positively affect teachers' sense that they can promote worthwhile change in their workplaces (Conley, 1991; Smith, 1993).

Organizational Health

Advocates of the debureaucratization of educational systems have contended that moving decisions to local sites will result in better functioning schools. They assert that this change will (a) enable individual institutions to be more responsive to their constituents (Brown, 1990; Chapman & Boyd, 1986; Clune & White, 1988; Malen et al., 1989); (b) enhance the ability of schools to embrace helpful innovations (Bryk, 1993; David, 1989; Garms et al., 1978; Lindelow, 1981); (c) promote greater efficiency in resource use (Clune & White, 1988); and (d) lead to more equitable distribution of opportunities (Brown, 1990; Bryk, 1993; Hess, 1992).

Research suggests that each of these possibilities has been only partially realized in schools implementing SBM. For instance, there are indicators that schools with shared decision making are more responsive at least to the interests of teacher participants in the process. There is, however, little data on whether or not these schools are attending to concerns of other stakeholder groups.

More evidence is available on the degree to which site-managed schools have embraced innovations, and it indicates that in this area SBM has fallen far short of expectations. Although self-governed schools do implement some innovations (Brown, 1991; Hanson, 1991; Strusinski, 1991), most decisions made in these sites tend to follow patterns established by more centralized agencies (Anderson & Dixon, 1993; Collins, 1994; Collins & Hanson, 1991; Hannaway, 1992; Hanson, 1991; Weiss, Cambone, & Wyeth, 1991). Similarly, SBM has not lived up to implicit promises that it will promote economic efficiency in schools (Brown, 1990; Clune & White, 1988; Collins & Hanson, 1991). However, in the area of "technical efficiency" (Brown, 1990, p. 247), the gain from a better match between energy and financial resources and site-specific interests, the jury is still out. There is evidence that "resources are [better] matched to school tasks" (Brown, 1990, p. 260); however, there is also reason to believe that widespread participation in governance exacts a toll in terms of time and energy from teachers, site administrators, and others (Murphy, 1991, 1994).

The notion that under SBM, resources will be better matched to individual site needs is linked, in some sense, to the idea that self-governance will result in greater equity in the distribution of educational opportunities. For this to occur, though, the decision-making structures would need to be sensitive to unjust allocations of resources and committed to altering this situation. Many scholars (e.g., Lawton, 1991; Mirel, 1990; Watt, 1989) have suggested that we have little reason to hope that SBM will alter inequities deeply embedded in educational systems. Furthermore, these individuals warn that the absence of centralized checks on abuse is likely to result in even greater gaps between the amount and kind of resources spent on middle-class Caucasian youngsters and on those who are poor or are members of minority groups. Early reports by Brown (1990), Bryk (1993), and Hess (1992) suggest that thus far SBM has not disadvantaged African Americans and Latinos, and that these groups are actually enjoying greater representation in decision-making arenas. Most analysts agree, though, that much more research is needed in this area.

Transformed Instruction

One of the central hopes of proponents of SBM is that this form of governance will contribute to "the ultimate goal of transforming curriculum and instruction in ways that increase student performance" (David, 1993, p. 31). Advocates argue that teachers freed from bureaucratic constraints and empowered to act in ways that make sense for them and their students will move to enhance the core technology of the school. With only a few exceptions (e.g., Bryk, 1993; Crosby, 1991; Goldman et al., 1991), data suggest that this hope has not been realized. As Levine and Eubanks (1992) conclude, "There are few if any indications that early movement toward SBM has been associated with substantial change in instructional delivery" (p. 74).

Several studies shed light on schools where SBM has failed to live up to its promise of favorably altering pedagogical practice. In many sites, the central governing body is the school site council. Here, it is presumed, changes in curriculum and instruction can be proposed, debated, and ultimately adopted if they make sense for a particular site. With few exceptions, research has shown that these formal governance mechanisms are largely inattentive to teaching and learning (e.g., Collins & Hanson, 1991; David, 1993; Des Carpentrie, 1995; Duttweiler & Mutchler, 1990; Jenni & Mauriel, 1990; Malen & Ogawa, 1988; Ovando, 1993; Wohlstetter & Buffett, 1991). Hill and Bonan (1991) nicely sum up the general consensus concerning local governing bodies with these words:

In many schools, the first years of SBM are dominated by contention about adult working conditions—labor management relations and fair allocation of parking spaces, telephones, and hall and playground duty—rather than by serious efforts to improve services to students. (p. 27)

Often the activity of site councils is reflected in formal school improvement plans; however, in some circumstances, these plans have been developed by a wider group of stakeholders, and the councils are charged with overseeing their implementation. In either case, analyses of these plans reveal that there is scant attention paid to technical core issues of curriculum and instruction (Wohlstetter & Odden, 1992). Marsh (1992) notes that many of the formal documents detailing school goals focus on effecting "changes in the lives of the adults at the school" (p. 33). And when pedagogy *is* addressed in these plans, the focus is often on additions to current programs rather than genuinely altering core instructional practices (see, e.g., Hess, 1992). It is therefore not surprising that most researchers have uncovered few "qualitative differences in the instructional techniques chosen by teachers" (Taylor & Bogotch, 1992, p. 17) in SBM and non-SBM schools.

Learning Outcomes

Most analysts agree that the ultimate test of SBM lies in its ability to positively affect learning. Interestingly, few investigations to date have explored the link between student performance and decentralized forms of governance (Clune & White, 1988; Weiss et al., 1991; Wohlstetter & Odden, 1992). However, the work that has been done in this area is not encouraging. Taylor and Bogotch (1992) found that self-governance in an urban district in Louisiana "did not improve outcomes for . . . students" (p. 17). Similar results have been found in Dade County, Florida (Collins & Hanson, 1991), Kentucky (Harp, 1993), and Chicago (Hess, 1992).

Some analysts have argued that the absence of positive indicators in the area of student learning outcomes is less a testament to the impotence of SBM than an indictment of widely used assessment measures. In some settings, efforts are underway to identify "a much broader array of student assessment and program evaluation measures" (Duttweiler & Mutchler, 1990, p. 42). It is possible to argue, therefore, that the jury is still out on the question of whether SBM is a reform strategy that is able to improve the academic achievement of large numbers of children. In either case, evidence on positive effects to date is in short supply.

□ This Investigation

Clearly, there is much work to be done if we are to better understand if and in what ways local control via SBM contributes to student learning, teacher empowerment, parent satisfaction, and the like. The findings we outlined above have done much to inform us about the possibilities of decentralized governance, and they have certainly pointed out places where SBM has not, thus far, lived up to the claims of its advocates. However, much of this work leaves key questions unanswered. Some of these inquiries relate to apparent failures of this type of governance. For instance, armed with current data, researchers might ask the following questions: (a) In situations where participatory management has "failed," was it actually implemented? If so, in what form (Bickman, 1987)? (b) In these settings, were there contextual variables that undermined the chances of SBM's producing hoped for changes (Miles, 1969)? (c) Have we given this type of structure enough time to reap positive results (Etheridge, Hall, & Brown, 1990; Rutherford, 1991)? (d) Are our investigations focused on too narrow a band of outcomes? Do we, perhaps, need to reconsider the goals of site-level autonomy and decentralized decision making (Collins & Hanson, 1991)?

Another approach related to school-level governance might focus on those cases in which positive changes have occurred in SBM schools. In this regard, scholars might ask (a) What are the management structures like in successful schools? (b) How does decision making happen? Who guides the formation of agendas and identifies topics for consideration? (c) What are the contextual variables that appear to be contributing to positive change? and (d) In what ways do these various conditions interact with decision-making structures?

As we contemplated these and other questions, we were intrigued by the possibility both of engaging in a study that would help us better diagnose the difficulties inherent in SBM and of attempting to better understand the conditions that facilitate successful local control. On the basis of the work we had already completed, we decided to focus our efforts on the latter set of conditions. That is, we engaged in an in-depth examination of an SBM school that is, by a number of indicators, successfully redesigning itself in ways that positively affect learning and teaching. We wanted to see what such a school looked like—on the inside and from the perspective of a myriad of participants. Our hope was to identify the forces propelling and allowing change to occur and to map the connections between these forces and transformed classrooms.

Given the emphasis on SBM in the Los Angeles school district, we decided to anchor our study there.[3] We then invited colleagues in academia and practice to recommend successful schools that were also site-based managed. One name came up consistently in conversations with persons involved in reform. Jackson Elementary School, a large institution located in a low-income area of Los Angeles, was heralded as a successful school by district officials, by faculty and master practitioners involved in the University of California's School Management Program,[4] and by formal evaluators of the city's reform efforts. Since becoming a part of the LEARN reform program in 1993 (and thus gaining considerable autonomy in terms of goals, plans, curriculum, budget, and—to some extent—personnel), Jackson's teachers have embraced several innovative, substantive pedagogical strategies that are resulting in observable improvements in student learning. After a series of discussions and written communications with Jackson's principal, its school site council, and the faculty, we obtained permission to spend as much time in this site as we desired.

Beginning in the fall of 1995, the lead author and/or a member of our research team[5] spent an average of $3\frac{1}{2}$ days per week at Jackson Elementary School. During the fall semester, we observed classes for extended periods of times; attended faculty and school site council meetings; regularly attended the gatherings of a parent group that had begun to meet on Jackson's campus; and engaged in formal interviews with the principal, the assistant principal, the resource coordinator, the parent liaison, and approximately 15 classroom teachers. We also had numerous informal conversations with the groups identified above and with students, parents, and clerical and custodial staff.

Data from these observations, interviews, and conversations were recorded in extensive and detailed field notes. These were analyzed in large measure in an inductive manner. However, certain broad questions did guide this activity. For instance, we continually looked for the answers to the questions noted below:

1. What are the management structures like at Jackson? Who participates? How are they chosen? Who sets the agenda?
2. How does decision making happen? Is it centered in the official governance structures or elsewhere? Do different groups deal with different types of decisions? What is the affect surrounding this activity at Jackson?
3. What about Jackson indicates that it is a successful school? What are the forces that seem to be propelling its movement toward exhibiting indicators of success?
4. How do these forces interact with each other? How do they interact with the governance structures?

As we observed clues that might help us construct answers to these questions, we began to map out what seemed to us to be pathways to transformation in learning and teaching in this site. Throughout this analytical phase, we discussed our ideas with Jackson's principal and with the school's lead teacher and asked for feedback. We also tested our notions in conversations with master practitioners who have worked for at least 2 years with the 192 schools in the Los Angeles area engaging in reform under the LEARN plan. These individuals possess a unique perspective on successful schools because they have worked with a host of institutions operating under a similar form of site autonomy. They have been able to observe both successes and failures and have developed important insights regarding factors contributing to both. Their reactions to our analysis also helped us to refine our emerging concepts.

In addition to this intensive on-site investigation, one of us (Beck) has had the opportunity to work closely with schools participating in the reform efforts in Los Angeles. In the summer of 1993, she served as a faculty member for an intensive, 5-week, summer training program attended by Jackson's principal and lead teacher. Throughout the program, she was able to observe them interacting with each other and with other principals and teachers, and she maintained some general notes based on her observations. Subsequent to that time, she worked with Jackson's principal during a

2-week, residential program for schools undergoing reform. During this time, she engaged in approximately four conversations with this principal (recorded in extensive field notes) and numerous informal discussions about reform, in general, and about Jackson, in particular. In addition, because of her work in this program, Beck was able to obtain a host of documents detailing Jackson's activities and progress under site-based reform. These and other documents obtained at the site or from the district office provided a deep and informative database to enrich the case study. In many ways, these data enabled us to paint a picture of Jackson prior to the time it became an SBM school and to sketch the early stages of activity during the implementation of this reform.

Ultimately, we concluded that, although SBM contributes to the organization's success in certain ways, it is by no means the cause of the positive work at Jackson. Rather, a combination of forces at this school have joined to bring about powerful changes in classrooms. The relative autonomy of the school plays a supportive role in energizing some of these changes. Other factors, however, appear to us to be of greater significance for change than does the governance structure.

In the following chapters, we discuss both our findings and the conclusions we have drawn from them. Chapter 2 contains a description of Jackson. In a series of narratives, with limited analytical comments, we describe the activities of administrators, teachers, students, staff, and parents—highlighting events and comments that are exemplary of this setting and that influenced us in drawing conclusions. We follow this in later chapters by describing four forces that seem to be central to the success at Jackson. Our premise is that these are the imperatives for real school reform and that improvements at Jackson can be traced, to a large extent, to the ways educators and others have responded to these forces. In the final chapter, we attempt to answer the question, What can we learn at this site that might contribute to the knowledge base about local control and successful schools?

☐ Notes

1. Much of the material in the first two sections is drawn from *School-Based Management as School Reform: Taking Stock* (Murphy &

Beck, 1995, pp. 11-35) and is used with the permission of the publisher, Corwin Press.

2. It is important to note that in a few instances scholars have uncovered "enhanced [parental] participation in many schools" (Bryk, 1993, p. 37) after the adoption of SBM policies.

3. Numerous reform efforts are currently underway in Los Angeles. The most prominent and far-reaching of these have occurred under the auspices of the Los Angeles Educational Alliance for Restructuring Now (LEARN). The LEARN plan, developed and endorsed by representatives from over 600 community groups, was adopted by the Board of Education in the spring of 1993. Under this plan, schools may participate when 75% of each of four "stakeholder" groups agree to do so. These four groups are administrators, teachers, parents, and classified staff members. Schools following the LEARN model develop a site action plan in which they identify goals in a variety of areas, including management, parent involvement, teaching and learning, school plant, and safety. Once this plan has been approved by a representative group of administrators, teachers, and parents in the district, the school is given control of approximately 80% of its budget and, under the leadership of the principal, is expected to engage in activities to implement the plan and to achieve specified goals. Under this plan, all contracts negotiated by the various unions are maintained; however, because all unions support the LEARN initiative, individual schools have had a great deal of success in obtaining waivers from the unions. Similarly, schools are encouraged to apply to the board and district for waivers if existing policies undermine any institution's ability to implement its plan. Thus far, the vast majority of applications for waivers have been granted.

4. The School Management Program (SMP) is a joint endeavor of UCLA's Anderson Graduate School of Management and Graduate School of Education and Information Studies. In this program, faculty members from management and education work with a cadre of master practitioners (many on loan from school districts for 2 to 3 years) to provide a number of professional development opportunities in and for school sites undergoing reform. One component of the SMP is the Advanced Management Program (AMP). For the past 3 years, the primary clients for AMP have been LEARN schools. A central feature of AMP is a 5-week, residential training program for principals and teachers of LEARN schools. During this time, these

individuals receive intensive training designed to assist them in leading their colleagues into self-governance. This summer activity is supplemented by 15 months of customized staff development—available to the entire school community and, at times, offered on site. After the 15-month period, the SMP continues to provide support and training to all clients on a limited basis.

5. We would like to acknowledge the contributions of Cindy Kratzer, whose thoughtful work in the data collection phase of this investigation has enriched the study.

2

Portrait of a Successful School

As noted in the preceding chapter, our goal in this investigation was to analyze factors contributing to improvement in a site-based managed school. We wanted to understand the forces (including governance structures) that helped this institution transform itself from what one teacher called "a sweet little school" into a dynamic, energized site. Moreover, we were determined to go beyond the mere identification of these forces. Our intent was, at one school, to explain how they worked and to map the ways they interacted with one another.

Because we wanted to begin our investigation with an SBM school that was succeeding in its reform efforts, we began by defining "success" and by identifying a site that fit this definition. To do this, we catalogued factors often associated in the reform literature with successful schools or with effective transformational efforts and set out to find a site exhibiting a fair number of these characteristics. We then moved into this site for 2 months, spending approximately 140 hours in classrooms, the cafeteria, and the library; attending weekly meetings of parent groups; participating in activities sponsored by and offered to family members and others in the community; observing informal and formal teachers' meetings on a weekly basis; and attending the monthly school site council meetings. In addition, we enjoyed numerous informal conversations with teachers, parents, administrators, and students and conducted a series of formal interviews with members of the Jackson Elementary School community.

In this chapter we present, in a general way, details of these efforts. Our discussion is ordered in the following manner. We begin with a discussion of three characteristics that, according to scholars, are evidence of success in schools. We then turn our focus, in the central section, to Jackson Elementary School, and we paint, in broad strokes, a picture of this community, highlighting events and comments that provided us with clues to the factors propelling this school toward genuine and substantive transformation. We conclude with a brief analysis of this school and of the impulses that appear to be nurturing the reform efforts.

☐ Success in Schools

Indices of Student Learning

Most thoughtful analysts of the educational arena insist that schools are successful when students are engaged in learning and growing in their ability to solve problems, to think critically and creatively, and to work collaboratively and independently on a range of challenging activities. However, there is not a large body of work providing rich descriptions of this type of learning. Indeed, the vast majority of scholarship that seeks to assess the impact of reform and to delineate the characteristics of success looks to scores on standardized tests as the important indicator of learning (see, e.g., Chasin & Levin, 1995; Murphy, Hallinger, & Mesa, 1985; Slavin & Madden, 1995). The decision of researchers to do this may be linked to the widespread availability of such measures in schools and to the fact that such tests provide a reasonably reliable system for drawing comparison across sites or between control and experimental groups. Several analysts, however, have questioned whether standardized, "decontextualized measures" (Gardner, 1991, p. 133) adequately capture the types of learning that are to be most valued. Lohman (1993), for example, points out that although such tests do an adequate job of measuring "crystallized abilities" (p. 13), they often neglect "fluid abilities" (p. 13)—the ability "to solve unfamiliar, ill-structured problems" (p. 15). He contends that this ability is a critical outcome of education and an important dimension of learning, and he calls for tests more capable of measuring students' abilities in this area.

Such tests, however, are not widely available. In the interim, we must depend in large measure on descriptions of rich and engaging classrooms to provide clues about indicators of students' learning. For example, Bryk, Lee, and Holland (1993), in their discussion of student learning in Catholic schools,[1] suggest that verbal exchanges, both oral and written, in which substantial issues are discussed are one sign of academic growth. They describe one classroom where "animated dialogue . . . [and] arguments . . . set forth, debated, and rebutted" resulted in "an air of involvement and satisfaction" (p. 82). They note also that students in this and other "good" classes had numerous opportunities to engage in thoughtful writing assignments and that instructors responded seriously to these products, not only correcting technical errors but also offering lengthy comments about student ideas.

Like Bryk and his colleagues (1993), Guttierez and Meyer's (1995) comparison of a traditional, teacher-centered classroom with two rooms that function as "communities of effective practice" (p. 50) suggests that the former is a place of recitation, whereas the latter are centers of developmentally oriented dialogues and conversations. They label these interactions as "responsive/collaborative" (p. 41), and the authors note that their purpose is to enhance students' "language development and understanding of content" (p. 41) as they engage with a text. For Guttierez and Meyer, a key component of learning is the ability to understand content, not merely to regurgitate facts. They insist that substantive conversations among students and teachers are both a means to this kind of understanding and, potentially, an indicator that students are actively developing as "meaning makers," adept at understanding and using language.

Theodore Sizer (1992), William Spady (1992), and Marshall (1995) offer another way of determining if learning has occurred that is arguably less process-oriented than following the patterns of dialogue and discussion in a class. They maintain that a good indicator of learning is a student's ability to seek out specific types of information, to understand and apply this material within a specific context, and to produce a demonstration or performance aimed at a specific audience. Howard Gardner (1991) and David Perkins (1992) expand on these ideas, asserting that performances marking understanding should not be limited to tests for mastery at the end of a learning task. Rather, they claim that demonstrations should serve as markers of growth throughout a child's academic career.

> Understanding is not an acquisition that clicks into place at a certain developmental juncture. As David Perkins has stressed, processes of understanding involve sets of per-formances—carrying out analyses, making fine judg-ments, undertaking syntheses, and creating products that embody principles or concepts central to a discipline. (Sizer, 1992, p. xii)

ransformed Teaching

Virtually all of the authors cited above insist that quality teach is needed if students are to become actively engaged in learning. B and his coauthors (1993) describe teachers in Catholic schools engaging in what might be considered "traditional" forms of pe gogy (e.g., lectures, drilling, homework review, etc.). They also ₁e-port, however, that teachers in their study felt strong commitments to their students as individuals and demonstrated these commit-ments by working with students on a broad range of activities outside of the classroom. Similarly, Edmonds (1979) and others en-gaging in the "effective schools" research often suggest that fairly traditional instruction, driven by a strong academic press and guided by shared goals, is associated with enhanced student learn-ing (Murphy et al., 1982).

Differing in fairly dramatic ways from the ideas offered by Bryk et al. (1993) and Edmonds (1979), a number of other scholars argue that teacher-centered instruction is not likely to encourage genuine learning for large numbers of students. Guttierez and Meyer (1995), for example, call for the transformation of teaching sites into learning communities where teachers build on students' prior knowledge and guide, support, and facilitate their construction of new ways of understanding. Similarly, Sizer (1992), Levin (Chasin & Levin, 1995;

Levin, 1987, 1991), Perkins and Blythe (1994), Schmoker and Wilson (1993), Tobias (1994), and others all insist that students must be active participants in learning and that this requires that their knowledge, culture, and interests must provide the foundation on which teachers structure new opportunities for growth.

Gardner (1991), Krechevsky, Hoerr, and Gardner (1995), and Perkins (1995) add yet another dimension to discussions of transformative teaching with their assertion that good pedagogy draws not only on students' prior knowledge but also on their learning styles and "multiple intelligences." This means that good teachers identify "strengths in children not typically addressed in school, and bring these strengths to bear on academic areas like reading and writing" (Krechevsky et al., 1995, p. 172).

Supportive Involvement of Parents

In recent years, discussions of successful schools have focused in some detail on the notion that good schools actively reach out to involve parents and other community members in the educational enterprise. The early studies on effective schools and the more recent work on school restructuring both draw the link between parental involvement and school success quite explicitly. In particular, the work of James Comer (1986, 1988) has done much to inspire recent activity and scholarship in this area. At the heart of his School Development Program is the belief that "shared responsibility and decision making among parents and staff" (Comer, 1980, p. 68) have a number of beneficial effects. These include the creation—within a site—of structures, curricula, and pedagogies responsive to the needs of students and the encouragement of parents to take active roles in the education of their children. Assessment of sites where Comer's model has been implemented has revealed "remarkable progress in boosting achievement test scores" in some schools (Wohlstetter & Smyer, 1994), and these data have helped to reinforce the idea that intensive and consistent parental involvement is a characteristic of good institutions.

In a similar vein, Henry Levin's Accelerated Schools Program stresses organizational structures that allow for "a broad range of participants and a collaborative approach in which students' families play a central role" (Chasin & Levin, 1995, p. 135). Research on sites operating under this model, like that done on effective schools and the School Development Program, supports the efficacy of creating organizations that encourage multiple levels of parental involvement (McCarthy & Still, 1993). Chasin and Levin (1995), Schmoker and Wilson (1993), and Wohlstetter and Smyer (1994) report impressive increases in test scores as well as improvements in other areas in three Accelerated Elementary Schools.

These authors, like their predecessors in the effective schools movement (Murphy, Weil, Hallinger, & Mitman, 1982; Murphy, 1992), see parental involvement as a means to promote student learning. Others, however, suggest that involvement should be considered not only in instrumental terms—not just as a means to school success—but also as a central part of that success. Lieberman, Falk, and Alexander (1995), for example, describe an ideal school as one with "a school culture and organization that promotes democratic values and that makes room for everyone to have a voice" (p. 118). And they are quite clear that "everyone" must include not only educators and students but also parents and other family members.

Heckman, Confer, and Peacock (1995) offer a similar, but slightly expanded, perspective. They maintain that schools characterized by (a) "equal and full participation" of all involved persons; (b) the "free expression of wants, wishes, and ideas" of these parties; and (c) open "public inquiry" around issues of concern to students, teachers, parents, and community members are instrumentally and morally sound (p. 192). Thus, they see inclusive schools, which welcome and involve parents and others, as both a means to better learning for students and an appropriate end for democratic educational institutions.

Using the Criteria to Select a Site

Drawing on insights from the scholars cited above, we identified three characteristics to highlight in our search for "successful" SBM sites for this study:

1. Evidence of student learning/academic achievement

2. Teaching practices that provide opportunities for active, engaged learning for all, with assessments that match instructional purposes

3. Parental involvement supporting the academic mission and indicating the development of an inclusive, democratic community

Interestingly, these characteristics coincide nicely with outcomes that proponents generally hope for when SBM is implemented. As we reported in the previous chapter, however, much research has been unable to detect these characteristics on a regular basis in SBM schools. We wanted to find a school that was managing itself and that also was successful according to our three criteria. In such a setting, we believed that we could get beyond correlational analysis, identify the various forces leading to positive outcomes, and determine if and in what ways these conditions interact with the relative autonomy of the site and with the participatory management structure. In brief, we wanted to know, first, if SBM was a factor in promoting success. If it did seem to be a factor, then we hoped to understand its centrality in the improvement process. We also wanted to know about other forces encouraging and inhibiting positive change and about how shared decision-making structures interacted with these forces.

Taking our criteria and our questions, we approached colleagues involved in educational reform efforts. When presented with our lists, most recommended a few sites to us. Jackson Elementary School was the one site that was most frequently mentioned as an SBM school that exhibited each of the characteristics we sought. Visits to this site and an examination of an evaluation of school reform efforts in Los Angeles (McKinsey & Co., 1994) in which Jackson was named as an exemplary reform site confirmed that this was an appropriate place for our research. As noted in the previous chapter, after a series of meetings, administrators, the entire teaching staff, and a representative group of parents and classified staff members generously agreed to allow us to study their school.

In the following sections, we describe this site. We begin with a discussion of the context in which Jackson is operating and move quickly into an overview of the school's history. We do so in an effort to underscore the facts that (a) Jackson is operating in an environment not normally associated with successful schools and (b) the school has changed substantially and positively in recent years. These points are important because Jackson's transformation coincides in many ways with its becoming an SBM school. On the surface, this would seem to suggest that SBM is a powerful reform strategy, that it is a causal factor in this school's change—a conclusion that many people in the reform community have indeed already drawn. We wanted to test this assumption and get beyond correlations and surface connections. Our intent was to examine SBM and school success from within the site, mapping backward from student learning, transformed teaching, and increased parent involvement and satisfaction to untangle the various forces shaping these dynamics. We conclude this chapter with a description of life in Jackson Elementary School today. In subsequent chapters, we analyze four forces that, in our view, are important in explaining the success of this site.

☐ Jackson Elementary School

The Context

Jackson Elementary School is located in a heavily industrialized area several miles north of downtown Los Angeles. Breweries, automotive repair shops, warehouses, and a neighborhood airport employed many of the parents of 1,170 children enrolled at Jackson at the time of our visit (October, 1995). The vast majority (92%) of Jackson's students are Latino. A number of these are children of recent immigrants from Mexico and come from homes in which Spanish is the primary or only language.

Many of the small houses and apartment buildings surrounding the school were built in the 1950s when a flood of GIs, returning from World War II and Korea, took up residence in Los Angeles, intent on pursuing the American dream. In the past half century, most of the Caucasian inhabitants of these homes have left, moving to the western side of the San Fernando Valley or over the Santa Monica Mountains into Santa Monica, Culver City, Mar Vista, or other communities for the upwardly mobile. With their exodus, the small row houses became homes to newcomers, not only to Los Angeles but also to the United States. Mexican immigrants, some registered and some not, seeking employment in the industries and factories, began moving into these homes. Occasionally, families purchased these dwellings; more often, they rented. As wages declined relative to the rising cost of living in Los Angeles, many of the families began to share their homes with family members and friends. Today, a two-bedroom home frequently houses at least two families, and at times, even more people crowd together.

Jackson's physical plant is fairly typical for Southern California. The main building is an older, red brick edifice with high ceilings and a wide corridor running throughout. This is connected by covered walkways to several new buildings that look as if they were once intended to be temporary. All of these are set on and around asphalt. During school hours, the central portion of the campus is frequently crowded with large numbers of children engaging in free play or in organized games or calisthenics.

Jackson is one of a number of year-round schools in Los Angeles, an organizational arrangement that in Los Angeles is primarily a response to, and effort to accommodate, rapidly increasing student enrollments. At Jackson, students and teachers are assigned to one of three tracks. Attendance periods and vacations are staggered so that only two tracks are present at any point during the year. Although this schedule has some advantages, it also creates a number of challenges for teachers and administrators. For example, because the total number of teachers employed here exceeds the number of classrooms, teachers are unable to "own" their classroom space. When educators are on break, their rooms are occupied by others. The year-round schedule also means that there are actually three official academic years at Jackson and that administrators and teachers must plan and execute three openings and closings of school each year.

The Past

Although we used many sources to gather information about the history of Jackson, one veteran teacher was particularly useful in helping us develop a narrative about life at Jackson over the past 15 years. She reported that in the early 1980s the principal, Mr. French, was an "old school" principal, part of the "good ol' boy network" that, by reputation, controlled the Los Angeles Unified School District. In her words,

> He ran a very "loose ship" in the area of curriculum but a "tight ship" in the area of appearances. He was very concerned about things like bulletin boards in the rooms and halls. Teachers liked him because he left them alone, and they

could do what they wanted; and parents didn't really know any differently.

In the mid-1980s, this gentleman was replaced by Ms. Burns. According to the veteran teacher, the new principal "really cleaned up the school," giving it structure and order. This administrator, a very disciplined individual who "really kept teachers on their toes," instituted several practices that persist to this day, such as a morning lineup on the yard with a flag saluting ceremony and schoolwide announcements. In contrast to her predecessor, this principal was very visible—"always out on the yard"—and knew every student by name. Teachers serving under both administrators reported that discipline problems declined dramatically during the Burns era.

Our teacher informant reported that under the second principal, Jackson was "a very well-run and orderly school." It was not, however, "very strong curricularly." Our respondent continued by noting that Ms. Burns respected her as a teacher but felt that she was too lax with her students. "I think you allow your children too much freedom" was a common comment made by Burns when she visited the classroom. (Two particular sources of irritation for the principal were the fact that this teacher did not require students to walk in perfectly straight lines in the hallway and that students were given many choices in classroom activities.)

Under Principal Burns, the practice of every teacher teaching the same thing at the same time became the norm at Jackson. "[She] wanted to see uniformity in all of the classrooms. She said that the classes should all look the same and teach the same things in the same way." The one major programmatic change occurring during the Burns era was that Jackson became an Eastman school. The Eastman approach, developed at a school by the same name in East Los Angeles, involves using a highly structured set of techniques for working with non-English speaking students and facilitating their development of English language skills.

According to our informant, "although the discipline of the children was very good under [Burns], she was very hard on the teachers, and the morale was low." Expanding on this, our respondent provided us with some examples. For instance, she told of taking a day off to attend the funeral of the parent of a close friend. When she returned, the principal quizzed her about why she took the day off and about who had died, finally concluding that the reason given was not adequate to justify a bereavement day. Thus, the teacher did not get paid for the day. She added, "When teachers were sick, [the principal] would always find some excuse to call them at home to be sure they were really there—that they weren't faking."

A series of events led to Burns's being transferred to another school within the district. This was followed rather quickly by the appointment of Leah Paul as principal in 1992. Paul came to Jackson from the district office where she had served as a Director of Instruction. During her first year, she changed very little at Jackson except, in her own words, "the attitude." She is a relaxed person, who believes strongly that good teaching can take many forms and who eschews rigid adherence to any particular model. At the same time, she does not believe that any approach is okay. In several conversations, she revealed that learning about learning was something of a passion for her and that her "research" had helped her identify her own "values about teaching and learning." For Paul, these values emphasize "a constructivist approach that builds on students' knowledge and engages them at every level." She places a premium on literacy—defined broadly as the ability to use words and symbols for understanding, communication, and pleasure—and favors activities that enhance students' ability to work together. Paul also takes great delight in the nurturance of creativity in teachers and students. When she came to Jackson, she did not criticize the previous principal or the ways things were being done. She did, however, praise teachers whom she saw using cooperative grouping and other promising instructional strategies.

Near the end of her first year at Jackson, a group of teachers approached Paul about becoming a LEARN school. LEARN, the Los Angeles Educational Alliance for Restructuring Now, composed of representatives of over 600 civic organizations, was created in the early 1990s by a group of civic and union leaders concerned about the quality and future of public education in Los Angeles. Under the leadership of former California assembly representative Mike Roos, this coalition of leaders worked together over a 2-year period to create a plan for reforming the more than 650 schools in the Los Angeles Unified School District. In the spring of 1993, this plan, supported by the leadership from the three unions representing school employees and endorsed by over 100,000 citizens, was adopted by the school board, and schools were invited to apply to become LEARN schools and to implement the model in their sites.

Participation in this plan required the support of more than 75% of teachers, parents, classified staff members, and administrators at a particular site. When applying to become a LEARN school, these groups indicate that they will operate under a participatory type of governance to develop and implement a school plan that articulates goals and strategies in eight areas: (a) mission and vision; (b) governance; (c) student learning, curriculum, and teaching; (d) health and social services; (e) budget; (f) parent and community involvement; (g) professional development; and (h) accountability and evaluation. Furthermore, the stakeholders at a site agree to be held accountable for the achievement of these goals, with the principal assuming the central responsibility for seeing that plans are implemented and progress is assessed. To facilitate the ability of a site to achieve its goals, the board and district give each LEARN school autonomy over approximately 80% of its budget.[2] Schools involved in this reform also have some degree of control over the hiring of teachers and administrators.[3]

Both teachers and principal Leah Paul reported that the initial push to join LEARN came from the chapter chair of the teachers union at this site, Sue Rain.[4] This individual remembered her early conversations about becoming a part of this reform effort. When she began to talk about her interest in LEARN, there was much apprehension on the part of the other teachers. "They didn't like the fact that the principal had such strong control in a LEARN school."[5] When they expressed these concerns to the union chair, her response was, "You don't understand reality. The principal always has had that kind of control. [Ms. Burns] had been a master of it." She would then continue, "Under LEARN, there is at least more equal control among principals and teachers." Furthermore, she would remind her colleagues that the first groups to sign on for a new program always get the best treatment in any undertaking.

As noted, the teachers then approached Leah Paul about becoming a LEARN school. At first, she too was uncertain about joining the reform initiative. Her concern, however, related to the time commitments involved. Paul had heard that the training planned for principals and lead teachers[6] required 7 weeks to complete, and she did not see how she could give up that much time. Eventually, the training time was reduced to 3 weeks in residence and 2 commuter weeks.

Although this would still be a strain, Paul wanted to respond to the teachers' enthusiasm. Furthermore, she felt that LEARN had potential, so she agreed to seek a vote from teachers and other stakeholders. After much discussion, the teachers voted, with no negative votes and only two abstentions, to become a LEARN phase I school.

The LEARN training alluded to above is required for principals and lead teachers of participating schools. Supported by the LEARN board and the superintendent of the Los Angeles Unified School District, the training was developed and is run by the School Management Program (SMP), a collaborative venture of the Anderson Graduate School of Management and the Graduate School of Education and Information Studies at the University of California, Los Angeles. The heart of this training is a 15-month program for school personnel that includes an intensive 5-week component for principals and lead teachers. Principal Leah Paul and lead teacher Mary Graves, after attending the summer training institute, initiated a yearlong process of collaborative planning that resulted in Jackson's LEARN Site Action Plan (1994).

Jackson Elementary School's Site Action Plan (LEARN, 1994) focuses on eight areas and provides a means by which the school identifies goals, articulates measurable outcomes by which movement toward these goals can be assessed, and maps action plans for most goals/outcomes. Our analysis of this plan reveals that it is quite informative, especially in conveying stakeholders' priorities. It also contains hints about the assumed links between governance and desired outcomes.

The first section of the plan specifies the governance structure for Jackson. This relatively brief, one-page discussion indicates that "the LEARN Leadership Council . . . made up of two co-chairs, the principal and UTLA representative, who are non-voting members," "10 staff representatives," and "10 parent/community representatives" will "by consensus" make decisions regarding "the issues and needs of students, teachers, community, and school" (LEARN, 1994, p. 2). Monthly meetings are scheduled for morning, afternoon, and evening alternatively to maximize the chances that persons with differing work and family commitments can attend. All stakeholders are invited to attend meetings and to speak to the council.

In addition, a number of subcommittees "formed as a direct result of an extensive needs assessment compiled by all stakeholders" (LEARN, 1994, p. 2) are charged with investigating problems and considering solutions and making recommendations to the council.

> These committees include: Curriculum, Staff Development, Budget & Finance, Fund Raising, Equipment, Staff Morale, School Environment, Parent Education, Hiring, Student Conduct, Staff Conduct, Professional Assessment, and Student Assessment. (p. 2)

The centerpiece of the Site Action Plan is a longer section titled "Performance Plan-Accountability" (LEARN, 1994, pp. 3-7, 11-13). Here, two schoolwide goals are identified:

> By June of 1997, a rigorous language arts program integrated in math, social science, science, and the performing arts will be implemented at [Jackson], emphasizing problem solving across the curriculum, acquisition of appropriate communication skills, resource development and interpersonal skills, and self-evaluation. (p. 3)
>
> By June 1997, stakeholders will be true partners in actively moving [Jackson] School from a place where children go to learn to a vital, active part of the community. (p. 7)

The plans for reaching the first goal are highly specific, focusing on improving learning by implementing several innovative instructional strategies, including Scottish Storyline, Mathland, FATHOM, Guided Reading, and Reading Recovery.[7] Another set of strategies attached to the first goal involves extensive collaborative and individual evaluation on the part of teachers. Attached to this part of the plan is an outline of ways to encourage peer coaching and an overview of a peer-review plan to be phased in between 1995 and 1997. Yet another aspect of planning for Goal 1 addresses the need for better ways of assessing children's learning under the newly emphasized instructional program. The Site Action Plan outlines a process by which teachers—working, at times, with parents—will develop, test, and refine a new progress report that uses "teacher observation, videotapes, portfolio evaluation, and parent surveys" (LEARN, 1994, p. 5) to better capture and portray student progress.

Detailed plans that outline strategies for achieving the second goal of bringing parents and community members into the school and of working together to make Jackson a "vital, active" (LEARN, 1994, pp. 7, 12) part of the neighborhood are also described. These include such activities as developing a Parent Activities committee (chaired by a parent coordinator); creating a telephone tree and purchasing "a voice mail Parent Link System to make communication with parents more efficient" (p. 12); offering "learning fairs . . . 3 times a year in the evening in the different subject areas, so that parents can participate in learning activities and increase their understanding of their child's educational program" (p. 13); providing English as a Second Language (ESL) and other classes; and bolstering family use of medical and dental services offered at a local "Family Care Center" (p. 13) housed in a neighboring school.

Other sections of the plan (e.g., professional development, budget, evaluation) are designed, for the most part, to support the achievement of the two performance goals discussed above. For instance, the discussion of the budget focuses on the fact that as a relatively autonomous site, Jackson expects to have discretion over approximately 82% of its budget. This represents a major change from previous years when the site controlled only about 16% of the budget and nearly all of this was under the purview of the principal. The major portion (61.5%) of the discretionary funds, according to the Site Action Plan (LEARN, 1994), will be devoted to accomplishing the first performance goal of improving student learning and will be "spent directly for classroom teachers" (p. 11). Worthy of note is the fact that

by analyzing the General Fund Budget with LEARN financial personnel, [stakeholders at Jackson] were able to add two classroom teachers—one, a bilingual teacher and the second, a computer laboratory teacher. The second largest percentage (17.6%) of discretionary funds is allocated for support personnel, including the following: Categorical Program Adviser, Elementary Counselor on year-round basis, Psychologist, Nurse, PSA, Health Educator, Psychomotor Expert, Computer Trainers, Bookkeepers for Categorical Funds, Community Outreach Paraprofessionals, Paraprofessionals. (p. 11)

Thus, these dollars are linked in a direct and tangible way to the achievement of both the goal related to student learning and the goal focusing on increasing parent and community involvement in this school.

Similarly, the section of the plan outlining professional development strategies is linked quite directly to the achievement of the two schoolwide goals. For example, it specifies that 1994-1995 professional development days will be structured to

□ increase the ability of teachers to use integrated or thematic approaches for instruction and to take advantage of the very latest research available on how children learn, . . .

□ assure that parents have support and increased opportunities to become more involved in their children's learning, . . .

□ develop real-life problem-solving experiences which can be adapted through the grade levels. These will include activities from FATHOM training, California Science, Project, CLAS training materials, and Problem Solving in thematic Storyline Units. (p. 16)

Other plans were to develop a peer evaluation plan, to plan portfolio evaluation and grade-level rubrics, to provide training in Guided Reading Strategies, to create a parent telephone tree and identify room mother activities, and to ensure that all stakeholders will have the opportunity to become more widely involved in the learning enterprises.

Our intensive investigation into activities at Jackson, which occurred approximately 1 year after the creation of this document, revealed that most of the activities outlined in the Site Action Plan (LEARN, 1994) have been accomplished—and in some instances exceeded—in terms of the breadth of involvement of stakeholders.

Jackson Elementary School Today

Visitors to Jackson Elementary School in the past year have described it in a variety of ways. A news reporter, after spending over a week at the school, used these words in her article:

At [Jackson] Elementary School . . . learning is fun again and the excitement is contagious for students, teachers, parents, and staff. This, they all say, is the way the public school system is supposed to work. (Kindy, 1995, p. 14)

A Jackson parent, Lena Ramirez, quoted in the same article, reported that

> two years ago she dropped her children off at the school door and was grateful to have Spanish-speaking teachers to converse with.
>   Now she sits on the school's . . . Leadership Council making decisions.
>   "It's incredible how they take our comments and they listen to us," [Ramirez] said. (Kindy, 1995, p. 14)

When teachers describe the atmosphere at their school, they use words such as "a sense of energy" and "very helpful, very supportive, very encouraging." Several with whom we spoke likened Jackson repeatedly to "a family." And virtually everyone gave high marks to both their teacher colleagues and the administrators. One noted, "I think most teachers here are learners. They're the teachers who try to do new and innovative things, not doing the same thing every year." Another stated,

> In hiring, [the] staff are careful not to bring on the old-school teachers who believe in the perfectly quiet classrooms. [We] want people who are willing to try new things and new ideas and are able to initiate.

The same individual described the principal as someone who is

> good at getting people to follow her lead without being forceful. She is able to convince people of the way they should go, but allows them to make the decision. Furthermore, [she] understands that the teachers have personal problems and families.

This sentiment was volunteered by many in the Jackson community with whom we spoke, and, interestingly, no one spoke negatively of principal Leah Paul and her leadership.

Students seem to think of Jackson as a good place, a place where learning is fun. Direct comments underscored this impression as did responses to a survey administered in the spring of 1994 in which approximately 80% of the students described their schoolwork as "interesting," 83% indicated that they "liked being at school," and 85% stated that they were "learning something new every day" (Kindy, 1995, p. 14). Even more revealing, though, are comments offered by students in the regular flow of activities. One teacher reported that while he was having a discussion with his fifth- and sixth-grade class regarding class rules, one student volunteered his idea of what could be done if someone misbehaved:

We could get them to read the books and answer questions at the end and do worksheets and take tests while the rest of us have fun learning about new things.

Another explained that they did research using computers, the library, and other sources, "so they could learn all sorts of new things."

What accounts for these reactions—for this enthusiasm about learning at Jackson Elementary School? Several people, including the principal, the resource coordinator, Helen Majors, and six teachers with whom we spoke, credit the adoption and widespread implementation of Scottish Storyline as playing an important role in invigorating this site. Scottish Storyline is a constructivist approach to learning in which the curriculum is organized around a narrative or a story. Within this model, the classroom actually becomes a story— with characters, a setting, a plot (including conflicts and problems), and a resolution. With teachers providing guidance and structure throughout, students engage in research around understanding and developing a proper environment for the story, in becoming the characters who should inhabit the setting, in solving problems, and in producing a product to mark the end of a Storyline cycle.

For instance, in one third-grade class in the spring of 1995, the students were urban planners and developers charged with the rebuilding of Kobe, Japan, after the recent earthquake. To fulfill their task, they had to learn about Japan's geography, trade, culture, and the like. They had to develop mapping skills and to think critically about priorities in a city that is rebuilding. Mathematics entered the picture as students used principles of geometry to map streets and to figure the space allocations for various enterprises. Learning in the sciences took place as youngsters learned about earthquakes and about the physical conditions that caused them and as they considered physics and ways to create spaces with stable foundations. Reading permeated all activities as students literally attacked the school library, using computers and books to increase their understanding of their tasks. Writing occurred daily as they filled journals, developed reports for the mayor of Kobe, wrote to individuals asking for advice or information, and prepared brochures and maps advertising the rebuilt city. The denouement of this activity came as teams of students, working in small groups to complete one section of the city, put together their various projects. Reporter Kimberly Kindy (1995) described the adventure:

> Wearing paper samurai vests and kimonos, two dozen third graders in _____ class squirmed in anticipation as they prepared to show their rebuilt city of Kobe, Japan.
>
> Each of six student teams had independently reconstructed a section of the earthquake-devastated city—using multiplication, division, and even some geometry to complete the urban planning project.
>
> "Here comes the moment of truth," said the [Jackson] Elementary school teacher as her student engineers moved the six sections together like a puzzle, watching as the roads and highways moved into perfect alignment. (p. 1)

In other rooms, students take on the roles of individuals coming to California in search of gold, of animals in a zoo, of astronauts or engineers in a space laboratory designing a special space station and planning its launch, or of persons recruited by the president of a newly formed South American country to assist in making a decision about the building of a set of factories in a heavily forested area. Most of the classes at Jackson are now using this approach (or some modification of it) during most of the academic year. However, teachers and the principal are quick to point out that, as powerful as this approach is, "We are not *a Storyline school.*" One teacher elaborated on this, noting that "Storyline is a good tool, but the important thing is not all of the fun stuff. The important thing is that kids are learning." Another chimed in, adding, "We don't try to squeeze everything into the Storyline. If there are things we need to teach— like two-digit division—and they don't fit into the story, we don't force it. We teach them, maybe in the same straightforward way we've always done. We use Storyline when it helps kids learn."

Increased energy in the teaching and learning arena is also linked, in the view of the principal and of the six kindergarten and first grade teachers, to the adoption of Reading Recovery. This is an approach that enables teachers to identify reading problems in young children and to remediate them early by intensive and focused tutoring. These six teachers, as well as the principal and assistant principal, are in the process of completing training to use this model. Their enthusiasm about it and their belief that consistent use of Reading Recovery will enable them to get all students who go through Jackson reading at grade level within 5 years or less have sparked the interest of other faculty. Plans are underway to expand training opportunities to include all primary teachers. New hands-on approaches to math instruction have also been heralded by several teachers.

Administrators, teachers, and parents also credited other factors for contributing to the excitement at Jackson. Parent involvement, for instance, has increased dramatically due, in part, to the creation of a place for parental and community activity. Under the leadership of a former Jackson administrator and with the support of a local Rotary Club, parents, working closely with the site council, reclaimed a storage building on the east corner of the campus and transformed it into a parent center known as the "Little Red Schoolhouse." This facility currently serves as a site for weekly parent meetings and for numerous classes requested by parents and provided by persons within the school, district, or community.

Students appear to be responding favorably to these efforts. Because of changes in California's testing system, it is difficult at this time to map improvements by standardized measures.[8] However, other indicators do suggest that children are learning. For example, in 1993, only 15 bilingual students at Jackson passed a state test that measures English proficiency to determine if youngsters are ready for an English-only class. In 1994, this figure had risen to 27, and in 1995, over 40 students for whom Spanish was a primary language demonstrated proficiency in English. In addition, teachers, parents, administrators, and outside observers comment on both the level and quality of learning at this site. For example, we were impressed by conversations with first and second graders in a bilingual class who had been doing a "zoo Storyline." Each student took an animal and engaged in research to find out more about it so that the zoo could provide the proper habitat and food. Several youngsters spoke to us about alligators and crocodiles and explained the differences between these two creatures, their native habitats, eating patterns, and the like. We then became involved in a discussion of mammals and reptiles and were told by our young informants that "mammals have hair and their young are born alive, and crocodiles and alligators don't do either. They lay eggs. So they are reptiles." One youngster added, "And mammals are warm-blooded. They can control their body temperatures some. Reptiles can't. That's why we put all the reptiles in an area of the zoo where we can carefully control their habitat."

There are also indicators that parental involvement and satisfaction have increased markedly. Enrollment in ESL, computer, CPR and first aid, and citizenship classes, offered within the Little Red Schoolhouse, is always at capacity. Large numbers of parents are on campus every 9 weeks to observe (and at times participate in) Storyline culminations. When, for instance, a fifth- and sixth-grade class created and launched a space station, over 30 parents were present as the lights began to glow in a darkened class while the theme from *2001: A Space Odyssey* played and the launching pad was unveiled. And they—along with teachers and students from other classes—listened as the student engineers explained the principles of physics that enabled a large object to take off and to be maintained in space. As noted earlier, parents also sit on the site council, and approximately 15 to 20 mothers regularly volunteer in classrooms.

Jackson thus appears to us to be a successful SBM school. Our analysis of it and of factors contributing to its success has led us to conclude that there are several forces operating in tandem at this site:

1. A commitment to learning that permeates the structure and culture of the school and that influences decisions about curriculum, the school calendar, hiring, budget, and the like

2. A strong and focused leader who continually supports and guides collaborative governance and works to create a climate so that both support powerful conceptions of learning

3. An understanding of this site as a part of a larger community (or set of communities) that shapes Jackson's interactions with those outside of its walls

4. Resource allocation and capacity-building efforts that support the schoolwide goals of improving student learning and involving parents in the life of the school

We argue that these factors operate as imperatives within this site in that they are the nonnegotiable driving forces behind the school's success. We also contend that these—not a particular governance structure—account for much of the success here. We do, however, credit SBM with contributing in several important ways to the ability of the school to articulate and adhere to these imperatives. In the next four chapters, we discuss each of these imperatives in turn, noting evidence of ways each plays out at Jackson School while situating our findings in the larger body of school reform literature.

☐ **Notes**

1. Although Bryk, Lee, and Holland (1993) conducted their investigations within secondary schools, we find that their descriptions of students engaged in learning are quite applicable to elementary schools as well.

2. Although the notion of allowing individual sites to have considerable control of their budgets has been endorsed in concept by both the Los Angeles Unified School District and the school board, the actual tracking of the budgets of individual schools and the releasing of monies to them have not been accomplished easily. Funding processes by which dollars are attached to and follow individual students are complicated by the fact that many students (in some schools, 60% to 80%) are mobile, attending a number of different schools in a short period of time. In addition, for a number of years, budgeting for this district has been highly centralized.

3. LEARN schools agree to abide by all of the contractual agreements negotiated by unions for teachers, administrators, and classified staff; however, they are not obligated to depend on or to follow district hiring practices. For instance, Los Angeles has a certain number of teachers and administrators who are designated "must place." These are individuals who have tenure but who have had difficulty working effectively in at least one site. If no school agrees to hire these people, the district places them in a site. LEARN schools are exempt from having "must place" teachers or administrators

assigned to them—unless the LEARN council (composed of administrators, parents, teachers, and staff members) agrees to accept them.

4. Leadership among teachers in Los Angeles schools is typically provided by individuals in two elected positions, the site-union representative, known as the UTLA (United Teachers of Los Angeles) chapter chair, and the lead teacher. In many schools, the same individual occupies both roles. This, however, was not the case at Jackson Elementary where Sue Rain serves as the chapter chair and Mary Graves is the lead teacher.

5. This concern, shared by a number of teachers at least initially, derives from the fact that the principal is given the responsibility to see that a plan is developed and implemented and that she or he will ultimately be held accountable for the achievement of goals. The decision to develop the LEARN model with this kind of structure was made by the LEARN working group after analyzing problems inherent in other efforts to democratize decision making when responsibility for shepherding the process was left unclear.

6. This training includes an intensive summer residential component in which the principal and lead teacher attend workshops and engage in a host of learning activities that occupy them from 7:00 in the morning until 9:00 or 10:00 at night. During this time, instruction and practice in team problem solving, budgeting, organizational analysis, meeting facilitation, and the like are offered. In addition, substantial time is set aside for the leadership pairs from each site to plan for activities with their entire community. Occasionally, a larger team of stakeholders, including parents and classified staff members, participates in the intensive summer residential program. Later, the training moves in large measure to the school site and involves both members of the school site council and a much larger group of participants within the school.

7. Each of these programs will be discussed in greater detail in subsequent sections of the book. Briefly, Scottish Storyline is a "way of integrating language arts throughout the curriculum. It relies heavily on children's previous experiences, provides children with real-life problem solving, and makes education meaningful to children" (LEARN, 1994, p. 3). Mathland is an approach to mathematics instruction that emphasizes creative problem solving in which the learner, often by using manipulatives, reasons through problems to discover principles and to develop skills (Math-

land, n.d.). FATHOM is "a 3-year training program for mentor teachers on effective teaching of an integrated, problem-solving based mathematics program" (LEARN, 1994, p. D4). Guided Reading is a strategy of enabling teachers to work with readers in small groups to encourage student reading and to enable teachers "to diagnose and remediate language arts skills" (LEARN, 1994, p. 5). Reading Recovery is an intense tutorial program aimed especially at kindergarten and first-grade students to ensure that they receive a solid foundation in reading.

   8. For a number of years, the Comprehension Tests of Basic Skills have been given to students in selected grade levels across the state. However, in 1994, a new type of assessment, the California Learning Assessment System (CLAS) Test, was administered to youngsters in Grades 4, 8, and 11. This test was designed to measure, with greater accuracy, students' critical thinking and problem-solving skills. It had a number of features that proved problematic to some parents and policymakers, however. After a major public campaign against the CLAS Test, the California Department of Education decided to suspend it as a statewide assessment mechanism. Thus, we have no consistent data on the academic progress of students at Jackson between 1993 and 1995.

3

The Learning Imperative

As we noted in Chapters 1 and 2, one of the assumptions about site-based management (SBM) is that if it is rightly implemented, it will set in place a series of processes that result in high levels of student learning. We also pointed out that very little in the research literature supports that this assumption has been borne out in practice. Indeed, most analysts of SBM are either silent on its impact on students' academic achievement or suggest that it has little effect in this area. Jackson Elementary School seems to challenge the latter conclusion, for it is a school where evidence of increased learning coincides with the advent of site-level autonomy. If the model we presented earlier is an accurate representation of reality, then we should be able to trace backward from changes in students' classroom experiences through teacher empowerment and improved morale and professionalism to the advent of SBM. Our experiences within Jackson, however, suggest a slightly different relationship between governance and student outcomes. In this site, a central factor promoting changes in achievement appears to be a passion for providing opportunities for what Newmann (1993) calls "authentic learning" (p. 6) for students.

In this chapter, we discuss the learning imperative that seems so central to this site's success. We begin our discussion with a description of the ways that people within this site respond to this imperative. In so doing, we note some of the meanings that surround the push for learning and that underscore the apparent power of this imperative at Jackson. Next, we consider in depth the processes leading to transformed teaching in an effort to identify the forces that directly and indirectly shaped this phenomenon. Finally, we examine the role of SBM in the promotion of transformed learning and suggest that it is a contributing but not a causal factor to this phenomenon at Jackson Elementary School.

□ The Learning Imperative

In the past 15 years or so, critiques of American education have been unrelenting in their condemnation of "a pronounced lack of interest of issues of quality" (Finn, 1981, p. 13) in our schools. This pathology, in the view of many, has resulted in schools that are at best doing only a mediocre job in preparing students to handle the complexities of work and life and to lead (or push) the United States into a dominant position in the world's intellectual, financial, and political marketplaces (e.g., American Association for the Advancement of the Teaching of Science, 1984; Boyer, 1983; Business-Higher Education Forum, 1983; Hirsch, 1987; Honig, 1985; Kearnes & Doyle, 1988; National Commission on Excellence in Education, 1983; Powell, Farrar, & Cohen, 1985)

A proposed antidote to the perceived decline in achievement advocated by the reformers cited above and supported by at least some empirical work (for overviews, see Murphy, Weil, Hallinger, & Mitman, 1985; Purkey & Smith, 1983) is the cultivation of "an academic vision of public education" (Toch, 1991, p. 56). Thus, the notion that if schools are to be successful, they must respond to an imperative to promote achievement is one that has surfaced in various forms in recent policy documents and other reform literature.

The Nature of the Learning Imperative at Jackson

At Jackson School, we were struck with the passion with which administrators, teachers, and to some extent, parents reacted to the press to improve academic life within their site. We were also impressed, however, with the fact that the push to improve achievement at Jackson differs in at least two ways from the "academic press" as it is advocated by a number of educational critics and reformers.

The first difference lies in the underlying motivation to increase learning. Many of the statements by reformers stress that we must "take charge" (Finn, 1981) if we are to produce disciplined, literate, and competent individuals capable of entering the workforce and of participating in efforts to recapture America's "dominance" in global arenas. Persons holding this view see schools, students, and teachers as deficient in many areas and stress the need for high standards, frequent assessments, and powerful incentives and disincentives to motivate otherwise recalcitrant individuals (Murphy, 1991). Furthermore, they tend to argue that "excellence in education demands competition—competition among students and competition among schools" (Edwin Meese, cited in Neill, 1981, p. 1).

In Jackson, we found a school where promoting learning was a clear priority and, for some teachers and the principal, "a consuming passion." It did not, however, seem to be motivated by the view that children and parents were lacking interest and desire, nor did we detect a belief that children would or could not succeed without a major push from educators. And the passion to improve learning in no way appeared to be driven by competition between teachers or between Jackson and other schools in the community or city.[1] Rather, it seemed that adults in this site took great personal pleasure in their own learning and wanted children to learn because being educated would enrich their lives in so many ways.

A second difference between the press for learning at Jackson and the picture often portrayed in the literature relates to its general orientation. Although almost all calls for reform are "cloaked in the language of increasing *student* [italics added] achievement" (David, 1995, p. 5), their rhetoric tends to focus almost entirely on the activities of adults in the schools. Calls for raising standards, tightening instructional strategies around a carefully chosen curriculum, and motivating teachers, either by improving workplace conditions or by instituting incentive systems such as career ladders or merit pay, are frequently presented as ways to ensure student achievement (e.g., Bestor, 1953; Graham, 1984; Honig, 1985; Kearnes & Doyle, 1988; Rosenholtz, 1991). Clearly, those making such recommendations are operating under the very legitimate assumption that teachers committed to high standards are important contributors to student achievement. However, in their zeal to promote better teaching, they sometimes fail to acknowledge the role of students in the learning process. Often the language and emphasis of reform literature suggest a very deterministic view of schooling (Corbett & Wilson, 1995).

At Jackson, we found a great deal of focus directly on children's learning and relatively little attention being paid to the adult educators and their activities. The Site Action Plan (LEARN, 1994) provided one indication of this emphasis. As we noted in the previous chapter, the entire governance structure is discussed in less than half a page, and many of the adult concerns (e.g., budget and finance, fund-raising, equipment, staff morale, school environment, parent education, hiring, staff conduct, and professional assessment) are relegated to subcommittees whose operations appear to be left to the discretion of members, because there is no further discussion of them.

Even more interesting to us than the lack of focus on governance was the perspective on curriculum and instructional strategies that we found at Jackson. This is a site where teachers are clearly excited about new instructional strategies. Most were quite enthusiastic about Scottish Storyline, with one person noting that the introduction of this strategy "changed the school overnight." Another described Reading Recovery as "the best thing since sliced bread." However, these same teachers stated over and over again in conversations that none of these strategies "is the important thing." Fred Summers, a fifth- and sixth-grade teacher, even as he praised Storyline for the way it changed his classroom, said, "But you know, all the fun stuff, the decorations and activities, are not the main thing. The main thing is that kids learn with this. This isn't about having a cool room or a fun class. It's about learning." Another teacher, who reported having a "great year" with a sophisticated Storyline related to *The Diary of Anne Frank*, reported that she had to "readjust" her classroom this year. When asked why she had changed when last year was such a success, she indicated that her students this year are very different from those she had before: "Many are younger and just not as academically strong." She then indicated that she shifted her approach to meet the needs of her current students. "The best, most wonderful approach is no good at all if kids don't learn," she said.

The Primacy of the Learning Imperative at Jackson

As noted above, academic press at Jackson Elementary School takes the form of an affirmation of the value of learning, a broad definition of this phenomenon focusing on processes that promote learning first and foremost for students. This press, or learning imperative, and efforts to respond to it are, in our view, the central forces that shape decisions, schedules and activities, and culture at this site.

Examples of the ways that the learning imperative shapes Jackson's structures abound. We were struck, for instance, by budgetary decisions made by the site council and apparently supported by teachers and others in the community. At one meeting, council members deliberated over ways to allocate the approximately $100,000 that they could control as a LEARN school. In what amounted to a brainstorming session, council members listed all of the ways that they "could" use the money. Because this is an old school, several of the items related to the physical plant (e.g., putting concrete in one rocky area near the parents' Little Red Schoolhouse building and painting the rather drab lunchroom). Some items related only indirectly to instruction (e.g., an outdoor storage shed, extra teacher and student chairs, a printer capable of producing banners); some related to material linked directly to instruction (e.g., a Reading Recovery roving teachers' center, CD/tape players, computers for classrooms); and still others focused on supporting professional development for teachers (e.g., stipends for Reading Recovery teachers who were paying for their own training). Although the discussion was far-reaching, the clear consensus of the group was that the vast majority of the money should be spent on those items that would contribute to the learning of children, teachers, and parents. This is not to say that other items were ignored. Although the council was willing to look for ways to cut corners on items related to the physical plant, such as opting for less expensive chairs or storage sheds, they did not have the same attitude toward instructional items. There was much discussion, for instance, of purchasing the best computers for student use and of taking care to wire the building so that these machines could be put to optimal use. And some items were eliminated from the list entirely simply because they were less likely to yield any sort of learning payoff.

We were impressed with the ways that a commitment to learning seemed to shape the process of making budget decisions within the site council meeting. We were even more impressed when we learned of the efforts to schedule learning opportunities for teachers. For instance, teachers in Los Angeles can apply to become "mentor teachers," for which they receive a small stipend and ostensibly can work closely with new teachers at a site. Every week a mentor teacher at Jackson, in addition to her or his regular activities, holds a lunch meeting open to all faculty and staff. At these times, issues such as student assessment and effective bilingual instruction are discussed, with the more experienced teacher providing ideas, suggestions, and resources to novices. The three meetings we observed were well attended with 6 to 10 teachers gathering to eat a quick lunch and to focus on improving instruction. Similarly, every teacher at this site is a member of a small teacher study group[2] that meets for one hour a week to discuss topics of concern or to engage in research about areas of interest. The quality of conversation at these meetings impressed us as we watched individuals wrestle with ways to create environments supportive of multiple learning styles in a bilingual, multi-age classroom, and as we listened to teachers attempting to understand the links between work with math manipulatives and the paper-and-pencil computations their students would probably have to make in the seventh grade. Even more impressive, though, was the effort involved in finding one uninterrupted hour in which every teacher could meet with colleagues. At Jackson, this was accomplished by having large numbers of students (usually close to 200) on the yard together for an hour three times a week. Aides, a retired administrator, and community volunteers—student volunteers who are off track[3] and parents—plan activities and supervise this large number of children in order to free teachers for self-directed professional development each week.

One rule of thumb among qualitative researchers in education is that much can be learned about a school's culture by listening to the conversations in the faculty lounge. Although Jackson does not have a lounge, it does have a faculty lunchroom where teachers gather daily. Almost daily as we sat with teachers and listened to them, we were impressed that learning—students', parents', and their own—was a frequent topic of conversation. Sometimes these conversations took the form of stories of classroom triumphs, and occasionally of difficulties. Most of the time, however, the discussions we heard centered around ways to enhance learning opportunities for students. We heard a veteran teacher advise a novice about effective ways to use centers and listened to numerous conversations about effective Storyline activities. We were also privy to several fairly sophisticated discussions about assessing learning, working with non-English speakers, and improving reading skills.

Also indicative of the centrality of the learning imperative at Jackson were the many informal conversations we had with teachers, administrators, and parents. The phrase, "the important thing is that kids are learning," was one of the first we heard at this site. And this view, in similar words, was echoed by many with whom we spoke. Principal Leah Paul's favorite stories relate to exciting things that the children have learned. She delights in describing how a fifth grader explained to her about the forces propelling ships into space. And she laughingly tells how one second grader, who had been doing an Egypt Storyline, came to school one Monday morning and announced, "They had *my* pyramids on TV this weekend." After recounting this, Paul invariably adds, "I love that story because it shows that she had taken ownership of what she learned. They were *her* pyramids and the knowledge was *her* knowledge."

Another teacher, walking us through her rain forest room, proudly explained to us why there were two different versions of the forest on opposite walls. "Here," she said, pointing to the south wall, "is the rain forest we built when we were just starting." Then, walking to the other wall, she proudly stated, "and here's the forest that we built after we did research on it and found what it was really like." Outside of the classroom, she continued, "It was so great to see them learning—not just about South America—but also about books and research. They're learning how to find information and how to use it to correct misconceptions and build better ideas."

The words of one young woman, a teacher at Jackson for a little over a year, summed up what seemed to us to be the driving force behind this powerful, sustained, and enthusiastic response to the learning imperative. Commenting on the school's culture, she said, "I think that people here think about their kids. I don't think they're caught up in, for the most part, showing their class to be better than the other classes. The kids are what come first." We would concur with this and would, in fact, expand her comments by making explicit an idea that was only implicit in her remarks. The teachers at Jackson Elementary School "think about the kids," about what they have learned and how they have learned, and this thinking propels them—individually and collectively—to discover better ways to promote learning at this site for every child.

☐ Forces Shaping the Transformation of Teaching

In what ways do responses to the learning imperative contribute to the success of this site? In our view, they are central shapers of the transformation at Jackson. The attention to instruction—especially the widespread adoption of innovative teaching strategies—seems to be the central factor contributing to enhanced learning for students. This, not the governance structure, appears to be the spark that ignites a host of positive outcomes, including enhanced teacher morale and professionalism, student achievement, and greater parent involvement. This is not to say, however, that SBM is unimportant at Jackson School, for many aspects of the governance structure contribute in important ways to what is happening here.

In the next sections, we present evidence to support our contention that the learning imperative and responses to it are the primary forces shaping success at Jackson. We do so, first, by considering an instructional innovation that, in the view of teachers, administrators, parents, and outside observers (D. Katzir, personal communication, April 23, 1995; Kindy, 1995), played a pivotal role in improving learning, transforming teaching, and creating a positive school culture. We then argue that the success of this and other innovations fed back into responses to the learning imperative, reinforcing the commitment that seemed to be so prevalent at this site.

Implementing One Instructional Innovation

Principal Leah Paul, resource coordinator Helen Jones, and at least four teachers told us that Jackson "literally turned around almost overnight" when they adopted Scottish Storyline. For many, this marks the event that helped to promote greater levels of student learning and increased engagement in school and classroom activities. Therefore, it seemed that we might learn much about the forces driving change if we could retrace the pathway that led to the adoption of Storyline. To do this, we had to depend on people's memories because we were not present when this innovation was first discussed. However, we are convinced that we have a reasonably clear story of how this event unfolded because the recollections of Leah Paul, Helen Jones, four teachers, and two outside consultants (one from UCLA's School Management Program and the other from the LEARN office), told to us independently, tended to corroborate one another.

Leah Paul remembers that she and Mary Graves, Jackson's lead teacher, heard of Storyline in a conversation with Jeff Nelson, a master practitioner with UCLA's School Management Program and a former elementary school principal from Ventura, California. Nelson's school had used this teaching strategy with great success. Both principal and teacher immediately liked many of the ideas connected with this approach. In Paul's words,

> Storyline just made sense. It was consistent with the way kids think—with the way they learn. I mean, who thinks in chunks of ideas or facts? Is that the way most minds work? No—most of us make sense of things by weaving narratives or plots.
>
> And another thing—Storyline seemed really constructivist. Kids' prior knowledge lays the foundation for learning. They start with what they know and think and with their questions and interests. And they begin to *build* knowledge on that foundation. What a great way to go.

As the school worked to identify its performance goals and to construct action plans for achieving them, it was Graves who suggested that the teachers might want to at least consider Storyline as a way to go. They agreed, and in the fall of 1993, Jeff Nelson spent an afternoon with teachers, talking about and demonstrating Storyline.

Teacher enthusiasm for receiving training in this method was high after the presentation, and they expressed this at faculty meetings and to the site council. In both meetings, participants quickly agreed that any teacher who wished to should be able to be trained in this approach. Surprisingly, almost 20 teachers asked to participate. This posed a budgetary challenge, for Storyline training is expensive ($300/person for a 5-day session), and Jackson was committed to paying for this and for substitutes for any teacher who attended the training. The academic coordinator immediately began looking into funding sources. She wrote a successful grant proposal and obtained monies to cover the cost of this undertaking.

What seems worthy of note about these events is the fact that the site council merely ratified what was essentially a teacher decision and that the teachers were exposed to Storyline because the principal and lead teacher thought it was a good instructional strategy. The beginning of an activity "that literally changed the school overnight" can thus be traced back to the wisdom of two individuals who recognized a promising pedagogical approach and brought it to the attention of teachers.[4] It can also be linked to a commitment on the part of teachers and administrators to promote learning and to the teachers' ability to see that a particular strategy would help them in this area. Furthermore, even though the site council was informed about, and in a sense ratified, this kind of professional development, it was a teacher who wrote the grant to fund training. And Principal Paul was the one who made arrangements to free all interested teachers for 5 days and to find substitutes for them.

The adoption of other strategies followed a similar path. Often it was the principal who identified a promising instructional approach; sometimes it was a teacher. In all cases, teachers were exposed to these and given the opportunity to make their own decisions about them. The principal, although she had made no formal promises, was committed to finding funds to support professional development for teachers. She or the teachers felt free to ask the site council if there was money in the budget to cover any training. They did not, however, appear to feel that they must ask permission of the council or depend on it for funding. Paul and one other teacher spoke resolutely of "finding the money" to cover worthwhile endeavors through grants or gifts, with a fallback position that they would encourage teachers to pay for training themselves if all else failed. If the latter plan had to be put into effect, Paul and others would work with the district to be certain that teachers got salary credits for their training; and this, in the long run, would help pay them back for their personal outlay.

Improved Learning as a Sustainer of Good Teaching

Even though commitment to promote learning and a wise selection of promising pedagogies inspired the initial adoption of Storyline and other effective instructional strategies, observable changes in student learning—evidence that they were becoming better communicators and problem solvers—have sustained enthusiasm for pursuing new ways of teaching.

Fred Summers, for instance, recalls his first attempt at using Storyline in his fifth- and sixth-grade class.[5] He had created a letter from a local city council asking "the students of Mr. Summers's class" to create a health food restaurant for their community. Excited about this opportunity, the youngsters set out to learn about nutrition, marketing, cooking, advertising, and more with the goal of actually transforming their room into this new eating establishment. For instance, students designed a survey and administered it to their friends and families to determine eating preferences among potential customers. The tabulation and interpretation of these results provided for lively learning in mathematics and what Summers called "logic and problem solving." Analysis of recipes created opportunities to learn about health, nutrition, and the human body. And throughout, Summers created activities—writing, reading, mathematics, and the like—that built on the work children were doing as they created the restaurant.

At the end of 10 weeks, the students proudly presented customers (parents, other teachers, and community members) with menus that elaborated the nutritional content of food items. Servers took orders and presented them to cooks who prepared the food according to recipes the children had obtained or created. Customers paid student cashiers who made change and thanked them for coming.

Summers recalled with laughter how nervous he was during the culminating experience:

Can you imagine—fifth and sixth graders taking orders, cooking, taking [play] money, and making change? I thought, I've got to be crazy!! But the kids loved it, and I loved it. And the parents—you should have seen them. This really helped them understand about the new ways we were trying to teach, and they could see how much their kids learned. So now, I love Storyline.

Leah Paul, who was listening to this comment, laughed and added, "How many teachers do you know who can't wait to show their planning books to administrators? Well, it never happened to me before coming here. But Fred started it. He got so excited about what he was doing that he would come show me his plans—just to share them."

Other teachers told similar stories. Most did not discount the fact that changing their teaching was an effort, requiring a lot of training and new ways of doing things. But we heard few complaints about these things. Those we did hear focused on two issues. Some teachers who were being trained in Reading Recovery expressed frustration about the demands of the training process. Evidently they had a great deal of paperwork and reading for the class they were taking, and they felt that this took up too many hours and detracted from their energy for working with students. And one teacher was concerned that the innovations that were being so widely embraced at Jackson did not pay sufficient attention to basic skills.[6]

☐ The Role of Site-Based Management

Throughout this chapter, we have argued that the response to the learning imperative at Jackson Elementary School—especially the widespread adoption of dynamic teaching strategies—is a prime mover in this site's transformation. We have also suggested that although many factors are certainly influential, the institutionalization of good instruction here is occurring in large measure because teachers can see that it is working. They observe and delight in evidence that students are excited about learning and that, furthermore, they are becoming creative and collaborative problem solvers.

Although we argue that consensus and consistency in the use of appropriate and emerging instructional strategies is the central factor shaping school success, we do not believe it is the only one. Indeed, a constellation of forces (some of which will be discussed in subsequent chapters) has worked together at Jackson to enable it to make the changes that it has made. In our view, SBM has helped to create conditions that enabled these forces to emerge and to find expression in productive ways. In the following sections, we look specifically at the ways SBM at Jackson Elementary School has facilitated this site's ability to respond effectively to the instructional imperative. We assert that relative autonomy from bureaucratic constraints gives Jackson two degrees of freedom. First, relative freedom from the district's mandates has allowed this school to challenge traditional ways of measuring learning and to construct alternative assessments for students and for the school. Second, as an SBM LEARN school, Jackson has more control over hiring than non-SBM schools. This, according to teachers and the principal, has been an important factor in bringing "good people" into this school community.

Relative Autonomy From the District's Assessment Strategies

The Los Angeles Unified School District, currently the second largest in the United States, includes over 600 schools, serves more than 600,000 students, and has 50,000 employees. With a large number of central office administrators generating a plethora of forms, rules, procedures, and policies, this district has a well-deserved reputation of being highly bureaucratic. Many of the positions in this office have been created to ensure that the city schools are in compliance with the 7,000-page Education Code of the State of California.[7] At other times, personnel have been hired in a reactive fashion to deal with some problem within the city. Three sophisticated and often contentious bargaining units[8] have, through the years, negotiated various contractual agreements; many of these deals have prompted the hiring of additional individuals to supervise and monitor the implementation of settlements.

In recent years, most educational leaders—including the superintendent of the Los Angeles Unified School District; the leaders of all three bargaining units; and a host of civic leaders, educators, and parents—concluded that the educational structures in the city no longer worked and crafted the LEARN reform documents. One of the many goals of this effort was to recast the relationships between central administration and individual schools—with the former providing support and the latter identifying goals, constructing ways to reach them, and exercising greater control over budgets and hiring.

When stakeholders in a site apply to become a LEARN school, they openly declare—by voting—that they wish to participate in this reform. And in the past 3 years, when the school board has welcomed new sets of LEARN schools, there has been a great deal of fanfare with the superintendent, the board president, and other state and local leaders pledging to work with these schools to assist them in improving the achievement of every child in the district. These statements of support are repeated regularly and publicly at board meetings, at LEARN training events, and at annual LEARN summit meetings attended by representatives from all participating schools.

As schools, the school board, the district administrators, and the unions have attempted to enact new ways of relating to one another, it has become apparent that change is not going to be easy. There are a number of reasons for this. For example, changing the processes for financial record keeping so that it allows for the distribution of budget information as well as the actual dollars has been a Herculean task, one that is only now—3 years after the adoption of LEARN—beginning to work smoothly. Also, moving the norms within schools and districts away from a "compliance orientation" (McDonough, 1993) toward a more innovative spirit has been challenging. Principals, teachers, and district leaders find themselves struggling to understand what they are "allowed" to do under LEARN and what mandates must still be followed.

At some sites, the difficulties and ambiguities associated with greater site autonomy appear to have created a number of problems. This does not seem to be the case at Jackson. At this site, being "a LEARN school" has apparently created a sense of boldness and a spirit of risk taking that certainly support the supportive, nonpunitive culture we describe above.

One story told by Leah Paul offers insight into this phenomenon. During the 1994-1995 academic year, a directive was issued by central administration regarding assessment measures that were to be put into place for all Los Angeles schools. This was not an atypical directive in that it specified that certain quantifiable data drawn from a battery of standardized tests and from attendance and discipline data be reported to the central office and used to measure schools' achievement.

Paul, along with two other LEARN school principals, was frustrated by this plan. The LEARN documents specify that schools will set their own goals for student achievement and that they will be held accountable for these objectives. The three principals were not un-comfortable with the notion of accountability, but their schools' goals were not the kind easily captured by standardized tests. Thinking back to their conversations, Paul asked,

> I mean, how can a standardized test measure oral communi-cation skills? That's an important goal for us, because it's important to our student and parents. And how can it tell you if the kids are solving problems *collaboratively*? And what about research? We don't necessarily want our students to know the answers. We want them to know how to go after answers. There's no way that sitting with a number two pencil and a piece of paper can let you know if they can go to a computer and get on the net and find what they need to know. I know we've got to teach the kids how to take these tests, because they'll have them all through their school careers. We just don't want to confuse them with more valid ways of assessing learning.

Paul and the other principals expressed this frustration to the district official who was the direct supervisor for their school com-plex. She was sympathetic but told them that "Sid [Sidney Thompson, Superintendent of the Los Angeles Unified School Dis-trict] asked for this." Paul reports that she replied to this by saying, "Well, just have Sid give me a call, and I'll explain to him why this doesn't work for us. I mean, after all, we're LEARN schools."

With laughter, Paul stated that "Sid was completely on our side." She continued, "A lot of the directives are just part of this system, but he is supportive of LEARN. We just had to demonstrate that we were achieving our goals." She added, "And we need to work with you all [professors at UCLA] to be sure that we develop assessment tools that let us know what we're doing and where we're falling short."

Paul believes that the willingness of the staff to commit to pur-suing innovative instructional strategies to cultivate a spirit of in-quiry, problem-solving skills, and collaborative work habits is at least partially a function of the fact that teachers feel confident that they and their children will be evaluated fairly.

> It's hard enough to take risks, but it's almost impossible if you feel like you're going to be on the front page of the *L.A.*

Times for low test scores. Everybody sees that and assumes you're doing a terrible job. No one asks about the things you are doing. They never find out that Jose is helping younger students use computers to get information or that Maria wants to be an engineer after rebuilding Kobe, Japan.

We certainly accept Paul's view that having a measure of autonomy from centralized accountability systems is beneficial at this site. Our experiences with administrators and teachers confirm that it is demoralizing to have critics assume that test scores tell the full story of a school's successes or failures. However, our analysis of the data leads us to argue that the morale-building impact of autonomy is only indirectly connected to school success at Jackson and that major and effective changes in instruction are much more directly responsible for the success of students at Jackson. It may be that teachers' willingness to try new kinds of teaching and to aim for rich and multifaceted student learning could be stifled by district controls. This does not mean, however, that, absent an educational agenda—or what Wohlstetter and Odden (1992) refer to as an "instructional guidance mechanism" (p. 9)—the relaxing of those controls will produce teacher morale, innovative instruction, and improved learning.

Greater Control Over Hiring

One other aspect of SBM (as it is defined by the LEARN documents) that has contributed, to some extent, to this site's success is the ability to exercise a large measure of control over hiring.[9] We make this argument because much that is exciting at this site seems to be linked fairly directly to the quality of the teaching force and because one third of the teachers joined Jackson's faculty after it became an SBM school.

As we noted earlier, participating in professional development activities above and beyond those specified in the contract is strictly voluntary at this site. Yet more than 20 teachers initially asked to receive Scottish Storyline training. Since that time, more teachers (including one individual who was planning to retire in less than a year) have also asked to participate in this activity, and those who went through early training are now clamoring for more in-depth work in this area. The same scenario has been repeated with Reading Recovery, with all of the kindergarten teachers voluntarily going through training in this approach.

We also observed teachers who go out of their way to help each other. One relatively new teacher joked that sometimes she did not ask for help "because I get so much." She then added that this actually meant a great deal to her—that her colleagues were amazingly generous, not only with ideas but also with materials. This sharing is especially impressive because many of the materials have been purchased by teachers out of their own funds.

Teachers suggested to us that this willingness to go above and beyond their normal duties is linked to the fact that people working in this school seem to share many views and values. Two newcomers to Jackson reported that they had interviewed at a number of schools when they were being hired, and one indicated that she had engaged in "extensive research" before making a decision about which offer to accept. Both commented that there was a special quality—a "sense of energy"—that they liked at Jackson. And both indicated that this was the kind of school they wanted.

Since becoming a LEARN school, the hiring of new faculty members has been handled by the LEARN site council who depend almost entirely on recommendations from a committee of teachers. Committee members, council members, and those who went through this process indicated that they thought it was an important contributor to Jackson's success. Principal Paul was also quite enthusiastic about this as indicated by a story she shared with the entire faculty. She reported that 1 week before her vacation, a teacher came to her and said she needed to transfer to a school with a traditional (September to June) calendar because of her daughter's schedule. Paul called the downtown office to request a list of possible candidates but described those on the list as "lackluster." Before leaving, she asked the personnel committee to "pick a teacher and hire her." Evidently someone at Jackson knew of a mentor teacher who "would fit the profile of Jackson teachers." This person, working with the committee, contacted this woman, recruited her to Jackson, and the site council hired her—all while the principal was on vacation. The reactions of the faculty indicated their pleasure over the entire process. They appeared to think that the ability to bring new teachers on board who could work well with them was quite important, and we concur.

□ Conclusions

Our time at Jackson Elementary School has convinced us that transformations in instruction have done much to contribute to the school's success. There are several factors that seem to contribute directly to these changes. Three of these predate the advent of SBM. One is a strong and passionate commitment to an expansive notion of learning—one that emphasizes problem solving, research, creativity, technology, collaborative work, broad conceptions of literacy, and communication. A second factor is an orientation that stresses student development rather than adult activities—an orientation that assumes that good teaching is not an end in itself and that it occurs only when youngsters are learning. Another factor that appears to be central to Jackson's success is the reality that the instructional strategies (such as Scottish Storyline, Reading Recover, and Mathland) work well in this site. They match students' interests and needs in ways that are producing visible evidence of powerful learning. Administrators and teachers at this site were able to recognize that these approaches were good ones—pedagogically sound and appropriate for this site.

At the same time, we cannot find much evidence that these educators were inspired to honor their commitments and to pursue innovations because of the presence of SBM. Even the fact that the school was able to pay for teachers receiving training in Scottish Storyline is not directly attributable to SBM and to teachers', parents', and administrators' control over the budget. In this case, the teacher who is serving as academic coordinator wrote a proposal and obtained $20,000 through a grant to support this form of professional development.

The autonomy of this site did not, in actuality, directly influence either the antecedent conditions or the provision of training in good instructional approaches. The fact that this school is site-managed did, however, support the ability of teachers and administrators to confidently act on their instincts, values, and ideas. It did so literally and symbolically by relaxing the control of the district bureaucracy over this site in two areas. SBM enabled Jackson's principal to negotiate the right to establish school accountability measures consistent with Jackson's goals. It also gave educators at the site more control to hire colleagues whose educational values were consistent with the mission of the school.

□ Notes

1. Only once did we hear mentioned the fact that the general public frequently judges schools on their standardized test scores. And even then, the statement was a part of a larger discussion about wanting people to recognize that there are better kinds of learning than those usually captured by such tests.

2. These meetings were called "Collaborative Planning Meetings." However, in our view, such a label does not capture what went on, at least during the three we observed. Teachers engaged in some planning, but there was much substantive discussion of curriculum and pedagogy, and it appeared that professional development was occurring.

3. In year-round schools in Los Angeles, students are divided into three or four "tracks." Each track has a different academic year so that at any point in time, some portion of the student body is not in attendance or is "off track." This is analogous to summer vacation in schools on a traditional calendar. In recent years, Jackson developed a Future Teachers Program, which allows and encourages fifth- and sixth-grade students who are on their break to assist teachers and teacher aides. In addition to benefiting students and teachers, this program assists parents who work and who lack the financial resources to provide day care for children who are not in school.

4. Paul has an indirect style of instructional leadership in that she seeks to expose teachers who command their colleagues' respect to the pedagogies and curricula she considers most promising. To the best of our knowledge, each time she has done this, those teachers have been the ones who have "sold" the rest of the faculty on promising strategies.

5. A number of classes at Jackson are multi-age. One teacher informed us that this way of grouping was instituted approximately 3 years ago when many teachers expressed interest in it. According to our informant, teachers can choose whether they want to teach a single grade level or a multi-age class, and administrators attempt to accommodate their interests.

6. In the same conversation, this teacher indicated that she felt very positive, though, about the fact that "no one forced her to abandon basic skills" and that indeed her teaching (which seemed to be quite fine) was more traditional than that of her colleagues. In

Chapter 4, we discuss the fact that teachers at this school have much professional autonomy.

7. Recently, policymakers have engaged in some debate about the actual length of the state's Education Code. The 7,000-page figure was given by Mark Slavkin, president of the Los Angeles School Board, in an editorial in the *Los Angeles Times* (Slavkin, 1995). A rebuttal to Slavkin's editorial asserted that this was an inflated figure and that the actual substantive portion of the code was contained in less than 100 pages (Hume, 1996). In any case, most educators believe that the code is unwieldy and that it limits their ability to respond to the needs of their school sites. This view is shared by State Superintendent of Education Delaine Eastin, who is seeking to create "challenge districts." In these districts, she proposes to waive much of the Education Code if districts implement plans that result in demonstrable and steady improvement of student learning (Eastin, 1995).

8. These units are the Association of Administrators of Los Angeles (AALA), the United Teachers of Los Angeles (UTLA), and Service Employees Int'l, Local 99, the bargaining unit for classified staff.

9. In Chapter 5, we point out that two teachers also praised the hiring strategies of the administrator prior to Jackson. They believed that her tight control over the process ensured that people who joined the faculty were what one called "a good match" for this school. We have no reason to doubt that this was the case and are not denigrating previous hiring patterns. It is important to note, though, that under LEARN, Jackson and all LEARN schools have the freedom and the ability to choose teachers not on the district's list of candidates. They also have the right to refuse to hire tenured teachers with seniority if they do not believe they are right for the school. Also, before Leah Paul's arrival at Jackson, the principal controlled hiring. As an SBM school and with Paul's support, all personnel decisions are now handled by the site council.

4

The Leadership Imperative

Since the early part of this century, school management practices have been built, to a large extent, around the notion that a strong principal is central to school success. To be sure, definitions of success have varied, and thus the specific strengths valued in administrators have also shifted over time (see Beck & Murphy, 1993). However, until recently, a consistent thread in educational literature has been the importance of an administrator who serves as a chief executive overseeing the production of a good school.

With the advent of site-based management (SBM) and shared decision making, this focus on the single person leading a school has waned, replaced by notions of structures that allow many individuals—representing all stakeholder groups—to share the responsibilities of decision making, management, and leadership. Research on efforts to implement SBM indicates that the shift from a single person as central administrator to management by a group (however constituted) has, in many instances, not gone smoothly. For example,

Lindle (1992) reports that in Kentucky the perception of many participants in SBM schools was that the site councils supposedly engaging in shared decision making were actually just rubber stamping
"what the principal wanted" (p. 22; see also Brown & Lindle, 1995).

Other reports, such as those offered by Conway and Calzi (1995),
David (1995), Geraci (1995), and J. T. Murphy (1989), indicate that in
other circumstances, groups of decision makers do become active in
governance but with less than ideal results. Conway and Calzi, for
instance, provide several examples of incidents in which a group of
teachers becomes a kind of "equity regime" (Wildavsky, 1989, cited
in Conway & Calzi, 1995, p. 47), a group of "equals" who control the
decision-making processes, often using it to serve their own interests.
David (1995), drawing in turn on Murphy, cautions that shared
decision making in the absence of "a strong center" can result in
"anarchy" (p. 7). Writing from the perspective of a teacher and a
participant in an SBM team, Geraci (1995) notes many problems
associated with this form of governance, including problems with
agenda setting, lack of knowledge about use of data and educational
issues or both, and the inability of SBM teams to ensure that decisions
will be implemented. And Guskey and Peterson (1995) remind us
that even councils that do make decisions for a school site usually
have little impact on learning and teaching in a school.[1]

The literature cited above and that produced by others (e.g.,
Bryk, 1993; Carnoy & MacDonnell, 1990; Clune & White, 1988; David,
1989; Etheridge, Hall, & Brown, 1990; Garms, Guthrie, & Pierce, 1978;
"Notes From the Field," 1991; Pacific Region Educational Laboratory,
1992; Rutherford, 1991; Smith, 1993; Wagstaff & Reyes, 1993; Weiss,
1998; Weiss & Cambone, 1993; Wohlstetter & Odden, 1992) under-
scores the importance of effective forms of leadership if SBM is to
succeed. Our investigation at Jackson confirmed that within this
school, leadership exercised by many individuals is an important
contributor both to the success of site level governance and to the
positive transformation that appears to be occurring. We found
limited evidence that, for certain individuals, shared, on-site decision
making helped them to have a sense that they could be among those
responding to the leadership imperative. Most of the time, it simply
created the conditions for people to respond to the imperative to
exercise leadership.

In this chapter, we discuss responses to the leadership imperative
at Jackson Elementary School and suggest ways that these interact

with the commitment to learning and excellent instruction discussed in Chapter 3 and with the SBM processes. Our discussion is ordered in the following way. The first three sections examine leadership as it is manifested by the principal, by teachers, and by parents. In the final section, we explore the interrelationships between leadership, responses to the learning imperative, and site-level autonomy, and we conclude with musings about the ways that these various phenomena interact to encourage school success.

☐ The Principal as Leader

Under the LEARN plan, the school principal is ultimately responsible for overseeing shared decision making at a school site and for ensuring that all stakeholders are, indeed, represented when key issues are being discussed. Furthermore, the principal is the person who is ultimately accountable for the implementation of a school's site action plan and for the achievement of the specified goals. Under the LEARN plan, the principal is expected to remain at a site for at least 5 years although there does exist a grievance process whereby teachers, parents, and classified staff members can file complaints about an administrator and, ultimately, if a majority within all of these groups agree, can ask the principal to leave the site. Thus, principals in these schools are in an interesting position in that they are responsible for carrying out a plan and accountable for achieving goals that must be set by a group of stakeholders (see Hallinger, Murphy, & Hausman, 1992; Louis & Murphy, 1994; and Murphy, 1994, for discussion of the phenomenon).

Some principals in Los Angeles (Jackson, 1996; Lawrence, 1996) along with administrators in other sites (e.g., Alexander, 1992; Lindle, Gale, & Currywhite, 1994; Robertson & Briggs, 1995; Weiss, Cambone, & Wyeth, 1992), have expressed frustration over what they perceive to be the ambiguity of their role under SBM. On the one hand, they feel that they are under greater pressure with this form of governance and that they are more likely to be blamed for failures than they were under a centralized structure (Murphy, 1994). On the other hand, these principals assert that they are accountable but not in control—that in essence, they will be blamed for bad decisions reached by the site council, for ineffective implementation by teachers, and, ultimately, for low levels of student achievement.

Principal Leah Paul at Jackson Elementary, in contrast to those discussed above, appears to embrace the ambiguity associated with her role and to use the inherent lack of definition to create consciously her way of responding to the leadership imperative. Three aspects of her style and behavior seem to be especially important in Jackson Elementary School's success. First, Paul is a leader whose prime concern is teaching and learning at Jackson. Second, she has clear ideas about many things and is quite adept at creating situations where others come to share her views and to work with her on key goals. And finally, she is a leader who does this by relinquishing much of the formal and official accoutrements of control.

Leading by Focusing on Learning and Teaching

During our time at Jackson, we had numerous talks with Principal Leah Paul. As we reviewed field notes and transcripts detailing these interactions, we were struck by the fact that in every substantive conversation, Paul spoke about improving and supporting instructional strategies that would encourage learning. Three themes tended to recur in these discussions. One was the importance of pedagogies that built on students' interests and knowledge and that invited them to solve engaging, "real-life" problems by seeking out relevant knowledge and developing useful analytical and communication skills. A second theme was the necessity of her personally taking advantage of chances to learn about good pedagogy and of providing teachers with time and opportunities to develop professionally so that they could work more effectively with young people. And a third topic frequently mentioned by Paul was the need for assessment strategies that could accurately inform teachers, parents, and students of progress.

We have already alluded to several incidents in which Paul articulated her beliefs about good pedagogy and the central role it plays in school success. Instead of repeating these here, we have elected to comment on several distinctive characteristics of her conversations about learning and teaching.

Paul received her formal training as a teacher and administrator over 30 years ago, yet her knowledge of recent developments in curriculum and pedagogy is extensive. For example, in one conversation, she identified several central tenets of constructivism, described authentic learning, and articulated the theories underlying certain pedagogies that purported to embody both. She then evaluated several recently developed teaching strategies in light of these conceptual constructs.

On another occasion, she discussed the teaching of reading, comparing and contrasting whole-language and phonics-based approaches and identifying ways both could be useful in the classroom. She asserted that using the whole-language approach did not mean that one abandoned any use of phonics. Rather, she insisted, what was necessary was teaching words in context using both whole language and phonics. "So we don't teach words like *hat* or *boy* or *run* in isolation. Rather we help students make sense of them by teaching students to read 'the boy in the hat runs quickly.' " She also discussed various approaches to mathematics instruction and offered well-developed views about bilingual education.

Not only did Paul reveal a well-developed knowledge of pedagogy, but she also demonstrated an enthusiasm for continuing to learn the best developments in this arena. Several things demonstrate this hunger to learn. During all of the professional development offered by UCLA's School Management Program to LEARN school principals and teachers, Paul was one of the most enthusiastic participants. Never missing an opportunity to learn, she especially concentrated on attending sessions that focused on better ways to promote student, teacher, and parent learning. Even more interesting to us was the fact that she participated fully with teachers (and as a teacher) in the extensive professional development linked to Scottish Storyline and to Reading Recovery. The former training took five, consecutive, 8-hour-plus days in which Paul, with teachers, actually did a full Storyline activity, learned the theories underlying this approach, and constructed and modeled this form of teaching for others. The latter required that she attend training sessions one afternoon a week for a 16-week period and that she do the homework and demonstrate competency in a tutoring situation where she was observed by several leaders of this program. On several occasions, Paul indicated that she felt it was "critical" that she and other administrators be fully knowledgeable about the approaches Jackson's teachers were using.

I know others might not agree with me, but I think it's essential that every administrator be fully trained in the best teaching strategies. How else can we fully support teachers? And I don't mean we just need to be "familiar" with good teaching. I believe we need to go through the training as teachers. After all, that's really who we are.

In the preceding quotation, Paul used the word *support* to describe her relationship with teachers. This, for her, meant not only providing opportunities for quality training but also giving teachers time to work independently and together on their own professional development. Examples of her commitment to this abound. For instance, on more than one occasion, one of us was involved in an activity that was open to principals and lead teachers from LEARN schools. Paul often appeared at these events, accompanied not only by the lead teacher but also by two or three other teachers as well. In a side conversation at one such meeting, she whispered to us that all of the teachers who were present had indicated to her that they would like to attend. She explained further:

I said, "Sure." And then I decided not to call and see if it was okay. You guys are always telling us that "it's easier to get forgiveness than permission." I figure that any time a teacher is interested in learning, my job is to find a way to make that happen.

We were intrigued by this attitude and a little worried that such a commitment might mean that teachers were out of classrooms and away from students too much. When we asked Paul about this, she acknowledged that this was a concern and then went on to explain how she attempted to support professional development for faculty without disadvantaging students.

I think one of the keys is to have plenty of good people who know each other and work well together. When I'm away, I know the school is in good hands with [Lisa] and [Elise] [the assistant principal and the coordinator] and with the teachers. And when the teachers are out, we draw our substitutes from other Jackson teachers who are off-track. We end up knowing the children and each other and our teaching styles, so that helps a lot to give the kids a sense of continuity. It's not perfect, but it's a pretty good compromise.

In addition to participating in professional development activities outside the school, Paul works hard with the teachers to maximize the professional growth opportunities on site. We have already mentioned how clever scheduling allows every teacher a chance to meet with grade-level colleagues for 1 hour each week. Furthermore, we have noted how the faculty meetings we observed consistently opened with a "quick teaching tip" from a teacher and how most focused quite directly on instructional issues. We might add that we were able to observe a 2-hour meeting in which Paul, the coordinator, the assistant principal, and the lead teacher painstakingly planned a yearlong, inservice program that was coherent, focused, and aligned with the needs of faculty and students. In this meeting, Paul was a strong, but not a dominating, presence. In particular, she tended to regularly remind everyone of the schoolwide priorities and consistently reminded her colleagues that their plans needed to reflect these.

During this staff development meeting, Paul clearly articulated another concern she had as an educational leader. This was assessment of students and teachers. Concerning the former, she asked her colleagues to help her "figure out" a way to assist students in taking standardized tests without letting these assessment instruments drive instruction. Several of her fellow planners offered ideas about this, but only one satisfied Paul. This involved devoting one afternoon to helping teachers understand the format of tests "from the inside so that they can know how test makers think" and to involving teachers in planning ways they could help their students become "test savvy." The other possibilities broached by colleagues, in Paul's view, "put too much emphasis on the tests and on traditional instructional techniques." She asserted that more would be lost than gained if they allowed themselves to be sidetracked by "teaching to the test rather than to student learning."

In another vein, she invited teachers to help in constructing a report card format that made sense for Jackson Elementary School and that clearly and accurately portrayed students' progress to parents. After a model format was developed by teachers Fred Summers and Susan Winters, Paul worked with teachers to write a request to central office officials for permission to use this type of report rather than the district form—a request that was granted.

Paul was as committed to authentic and productive strategies for evaluating teachers as she was to developing such assessments for students. Referring to the work of a subcommittee charged with developing a peer support and evaluation process, she remarked that recently they had indicated that they would like more formal training in peer coaching. She then asked us to identify individuals at UCLA who were experts in this area so that she could bring them to the school to work with this teacher committee. In anticipation of their success in developing this plan, she worked with the chair of the teachers union chapter at Jackson to ask for support of United Teachers of Los Angeles (UTLA) in this endeavor. Furthermore, she asked permission from the district to abandon the old evaluation strategies and to adopt the format the teachers designed. Both support and permission have been granted, and Paul and the committee anticipate having a peer coaching/evaluation model ready to be piloted during 1996.

Leading by Influencing Teachers to Choose Good Strategies

Often after visiting Jackson, we would talk about our impressions. Invariably, we would end up discussing the principal, making statements such as "[Leah Paul] knows exactly what she wants, but she leads with a gentle hand" and "That woman has great political savvy. She knows how to set things up so that teachers make decisions—but their decisions are very much in line with what she wants." Our conversations with Paul revealed that this ability was one she had, at least to some extent, consciously cultivated.

On two occasions, we were able to talk at length with Paul about the fact that her staff had embraced so many innovative and pedagogically sound teaching strategies in a relatively short period of time. She explained that she was certain that "nothing works if teachers don't buy in—if they don't feel ownership." She added,

And they have to know that you see them as professionals and trust them. This doesn't mean, though, that you shouldn't influence them. I think part of treating them like professionals is assuming that they want to do what's best for children and that they will welcome a chance to learn new things.

Paul then explained to us the advent of Reading Recovery at Jackson:

> I had heard about it and knew that it was a solid strategy. And it really is something we need. We can't let children get away without their being able to read at grade level. That's just critical.
>
> I took [Mary Graves] [a respected faculty member who had served as both lead and mentor teacher] to a presentation on Reading Recovery, and I had a feeling she would like it. Well, she thought it was great and talked it up with the other teachers.
>
> Eventually we asked if any kindergarten or first-grade teachers would like to be trained in Reading Recovery, and six people volunteered. And the district wouldn't let us pay for this since it's a real course for credit. They had to pay for their own—although they got salary points.

She continued by stating that this was the way things "seemed to get done" at Jackson.

> I never force things. That doesn't work. But I want to be sure teachers have a chance to choose from the very best.

In addition to setting up conditions where faculty members can be exposed to good ideas, Paul reinforces their wise choices by frequently and openly praising them, their courage in trying new things, and the ways they take "good techniques like Storyline or Reading Recovery" and make them work. She even finds ways to praise units or activities that do not work out as the teachers intended. When, for instance, one Storyline culmination did not come off as the teacher planned, Paul's comments to him were quite positive. She stressed the value of trying new things and noted all of the things students had learned, both from successful activities and from those that did not work so well. On another occasion, Paul expressed to us her belief that she was much more influential if she was positive and noted that she concentrated on praise and on substantive conversation and did not criticize faculty. "I guess I could point out faults, but I'm convinced that that does more harm than good—especially when teachers are working so hard." Faculty members also commented on this quality, pointing out that she treated everyone—students, teachers, staff members, and parents—in a gentle and positive way. Some teachers expressed frustration about her "soft touch" with students who had been sent to her for discipline. None, however, had anything negative to say about her positive approach with them.

We were struck by another thing Leah Paul did that, in our view, helped to reinforce the development of teacher knowledge and expertise around curricula and pedagogies. Because Jackson is recognized as a leader in the adoption and implementation of innovative teaching strategies, principals (and occasionally teachers) from other schools frequently ask Paul to do presentations on Storyline or FATHOM, the recently adopted approach to teaching mathematics. She consistently asks teachers to take the lead in doing these. We observed several incidents when this occurred and were struck, among other things, with the commitment, knowledge, and pride of teachers making the presentations. It appeared that they had done extensive work, demonstrating familiarity, not only with the techniques but also with the theories behind them.

Leading by Relinquishing Formal Control Over Many Activities

Much of the discussion presented above hints at ways Leah Paul persuades by relinquishing tight control over activities and people at Jackson, opting instead to influence, praise, and support others. In no place is this more evident than in meetings of Jackson's site council. According to LEARN documents, the site council is to include representatives of all stakeholder groups—administrators, teachers, parents, and staff members. The expectation is that the principal will be a member (and in all likelihood the chair) of this council because she or he is ultimately responsible for what happens at the site. Since 1989, when an agreement that ended a teacher walk-out specified that teachers would hold the lion's share of seats on SBM councils, in most sites teachers are in the majority on these councils. This agreement was not nullified by LEARN even though a small number of schools have elected to ask the union for waivers to allow an equal number of teachers and parents to be involved.

Jackson did not elect to ask for this waiver.[2] Paul, however, did instigate a change from the typical site council in that she and the assistant principal suggested that they serve only as nonvoting members of the council. She explained her reasoning in offering this suggestion:

> If we were voting members, we'd be two extra "administrator votes." That would mean that we'd need to add more teachers and parents. We'd have to increase the number of teachers because of the contract, and if we did that, we'd want to have more parents. And that would just make the council too big. You just can't work effectively when you have 15 or 20 people trying to make decisions.

Paul continued by pointing out that the whole idea of voting members is in some ways a moot issue because "we operate by consensus." However, she added, "It's important symbolically that we're [the administrators] not trying to control things." She also noted two additional benefits to her being a nonvoting member of the council. One related to the symbolic value of her visibly relinquishing what some might view as a sort of power. "It's an important symbol of what this new way of doing things is all about." A second benefit had a very instrumental flavor.

> I can learn a lot by participating in the meetings without having to be an actual decision maker. It's great for me to bring ideas to the group and to hear their review. If I voted, I might be more of an advocate of a perspective. This way I'm a learner.

Teachers offered a slightly different perspective on Paul's relinquishment of much of the control sometimes associated with the principalship. For Fred Summers, her attitude conveyed respect for teachers as professionals. In response to the question, "How would you describe [Jackson] to a friend or colleague?" he stated,

> I would describe it as a place where I feel treated like a professional. I feel respected by my colleagues. And I feel like

the decisions that I make are—they matter and they're trusted. When I wanted to go against the Master Plan of the district—oh boy, I'm putting this on tape—the Master Plan says I'm supposed to still be teaching Spanish reading to my fifth and sixth graders. I went to [Leah] and [the coordinator], and I said, "I know what the Master Plan says, but these kids are going to middle school next year. I am not going to teach them Spanish reading." And they said, "Well, of course not. You have every right to make that decision. You're the teacher."

Now our last coordinator would have hung me by the yardarms for not following the Master Plan. But [the coordinator and Leah] both said, "Go for it. You're absolutely right! We trust your judgment."

And I'm like, "Wow, what a concept!"

☐ Teachers as Leaders

At Jackson, an important counterbalance to Leah Paul's supportive, distributive style of leadership was the presence of a number of teachers who took on leadership responsibilities. At this site, we met numerous faculty members who, in our view, are exercising influence over colleagues in the school and district in important ways. In this section, we briefly describe the kinds of leadership behaviors and qualities we observed. We then consider, in some detail, factors contributing to teachers' development in this area.

Leading in the Art of Teaching

Leah Paul is not the only instructional leader at Jackson School, for several teachers also embrace this role. This is especially the case with the veteran teachers. Several individuals who had been teaching for at least 10 years and who had been at this site for more than 5 years frequently offer help and advice to new teachers and to the administrators. The recipients of these offerings of support seem quite pleased to accord to these teachers a leadership role.

Sometimes these veteran teachers possess a title, such as "Mentor Teacher," that officially designates them as experts and as leaders.

However, many who were not in designated leadership positions volunteer frequently to help newer colleagues prepare teaching units, address classroom management needs, and the like. Several things about the exercise of instructional leadership by teachers seem worthy of note. First, we were struck by the fact that veteran teachers are not hesitant to offer help, advice, and opinions. This behavior is evidently quite "normal" in Jackson's culture. Veteran teachers seem to assume that part of their job is to serve as leaders for their junior colleagues. Second, teacher leadership appears to be linked to expertise in a particular arena. Even though veteran teachers most often take the lead in expressing ideas and seeking to influence policy and practice at this site, other teachers who have some special knowledge and skill often step into leadership roles. Third, teacher leadership is exercised throughout the school day in multiple settings. Sometimes these are formal staff development opportunities, but more often they occur during the regular course of the day—in the lunchroom, the hallway, informal meetings, and the weekly collaborative planning times.

Numerous incidents that capture the lack of hesitancy on the part of veteran teachers to assume a leadership role with others can be cited. Most revealing to us were the informal interactions around issues of teaching and learning that seemed to occur so often. We have already mentioned overhearing a lunchroom conversation in which a veteran teacher was working with a beginner on setting up effective centers in the classroom. These types of interactions were repeated frequently at this site. We saw one experienced educator explain research about pros and cons of retaining children to a relative newcomer. Over lunch, another explained the value of using narratives as a central part of report cards. And we observed several times when those who had been on site for some time hauled materials from their room to that of a relative newcomer. Each time this occurred, the veteran spent some time explaining ways to use this material to maximum advantage. More than once, we observed what seemed to be an informal coaching session in which a novice sought out a more experienced educator, demonstrated something she or he was doing, and received tips about ways to improve the delivery of instruction.

We also observed, during a collaborative planning meeting, a conversation among a group of middle-grade teachers about appropriate art activities for the holidays. The thing that was most interesting about this discussion was the way the leadership of the group shifted depending on the topic at hand. Three teachers who had expertise about some issue seemed to alternate quite naturally as moderators of this meeting. A teacher who had collected a number of craft activities at one point was managing the conversation as she pointed out specific features of different activities and offered tips for making them go smoothly.

As this discussion wound down, another teacher assumed the role of leader as questions about the appropriateness of certain activities were raised.[3] Aware of the fact that several religious traditions are represented at Jackson and of the school's commitment to be "a community-centered school where all children are valued" (LEARN, 1994, p. 1), this teacher wanted to be sure that they were recognizing and supporting various perspectives on this and other holidays. She suggested that they think of ways to recognize Hanukkah and Kwanza and that they always provide alternative activities for those who celebrated no holidays. She facilitated a discussion around these ideas in which various teachers offered ideas.

This led to a conversation about ways to turn the making of crafts into learning opportunities for children. Here, yet another teacher took the lead and began to stress the ways that some art activities could provide wonderful chances "for kids to work together and to learn to be collaborative." She then steered the discussion in such a way that others began chiming in with ideas about tying holiday activities to Storylines—either those they were doing or perhaps had already done. One teacher, whose classroom had become Antarctica (in a Storyline that revolved around "Mr. Popper's Penguins"), began to think of ways she could focus on "cold things" rather than on specific holidays. Another, whose class had done a Storyline on Native Americans in which the students were members of two tribes, one on the east coast and the other in the west, thought about focusing on holidays in general and building on things the children had learned about these two cultures. Again, the role of discussion leader during this time stayed with the teacher who raised the issue. He was the one who noticed when one teacher had started to speak and been cut off, and he made sure she had an opportunity to be heard. He also was the one who, during this conversation, most often used affirming phrases such as "great idea" or "exactly" or "yes, that's terrific."

The incidents discussed above demonstrate our final point to some extent. That is, we saw teachers exercising leadership in all kinds of settings. Often these situations were informal, but teachers also operated as leaders in formal meetings that included parents and administrators. One recalled several times when "We told [Leah Paul] that we thought something was a good idea—that it would work for our kids." She continued by recalling, "Sometimes I think she was a little shaky, but she'd say, 'Hey, you're professionals and you know the school and the kids. Let's go with it.' And we did!" Another remembered several occasions when they had been in situations involving district officials, university professors, school board members, and other teachers and principals when "Something came up, and I felt like I had something to contribute, so I did." This teacher went on to say that most of the time she was simply providing additional information about some topic, "but sometimes I really thought they were going in the wrong direction."

Leading in More Formal Ways
Within the Organization

In addition to providing leadership around issues of instruction, many teachers at Jackson are in charge of nonacademic activities within the organization. Indeed, of the 39 teachers at this site, 26 have responsibility beyond their teaching. For example, 6 teachers (2 for each track) are in charge of earthquake safety. This is no small responsibility at this site, for Jackson is near the epicenter of the 1994 Northridge quake. Many of the buildings were damaged, and the fear and tendency to panic over small tremors (or even low-flying airplanes!) have not subsided. These teachers are responsible for planning and implementing safety activities in the event of a quake. This includes developing plans for evacuating the buildings, contacting parents, and preparing to do first aid. It also involves educating students and teachers about these plans and running at least one simulation "earthquake drill" during each track.

Two other teachers are in charge of the computers. Again, this is a major responsibility. Four years ago, computers were not used at this site. Principals and teachers, for the most part, were "illiterate" in this area. A few used computers at home, but none employed this kind of technology for instruction. Those who lead in this area assess the school's needs and capabilities and make recommendations to the site council regarding upgrades and additional purchases. They also oversee the training of teachers and parents and the care and maintenance of the equipment. Furthermore, they monitor the software that is developed and keep teachers and the LEARN council apprised of programs likely to benefit Jackson's students.

Another set of teachers serve as chairpersons of a variety of subcommittees specified in the Site Action Plan (LEARN, 1994). We have already mentioned Fred Summer's leadership in creating a model for a new kind of report card. Other teachers lead groups working on peer evaluation and coaching, on building a sense of community, on working with parents, on identifying and spearheading appeals to the district and unions for waivers in some areas, on planning professional development opportunities, and on supplemental services for students and families. These individuals are charged with monitoring the implementation of the Site Action Plan and with recrafting the plan, which is intended to be what Paul calls "a living document."

It appeared to us that teachers in these leadership roles really do have a high degree of authority in their respective areas. For instance, when in one faculty meeting a discussion of computer needs broke out, Summers spearheaded the discussion, offered explanations, and broached ideas. If addressing the concern required major expenditures, Summers indicated that the issue needed to go to the site council. Otherwise, he held sway as long as the focus was computers. We saw this repeated several times with other teachers as the issues changed.

□ Parents as Emerging Leaders

As we thought about the leadership offered by parents at this site, at first we thought it was minimal. Although they were present for site council meetings and many other events, for the most part, they deferred to the teachers. Language barriers (most meetings are conducted in English although translations are always offered); strong teachers who tend to be quite vocal; and a sense, expressed by two parents we interviewed, that teachers are the ones who "should" be making educational decisions are all factors that contribute to the parents' reserve in these situations. However, a more reflective reading of our field data and consideration of these in light of what we know about the history of this school community suggest to us that a number of parents are emerging as leaders at this time. Furthermore, it seems that becoming an SBM school has had the most direct influence on the development of leadership among parents.

Lena Ramirez, who for 2 years served as a parent representative on the LEARN site council, is a shining example of one such emergent leader. By her own admission, she was hesitant to speak up at the school, assuming that it was a place for educators to make the decisions (Kindy, 1995). However, with the advent of LEARN, this changed. Her story of how this happened, of how she came to see that she could be a part of decision making at her children's school, is interesting.

Leading by Supporting Teachers and the School and by Encouraging Parental Involvement

When Jackson became a LEARN school, staff, with the help of the leadership from the LEARN office, held a big celebration. This involved food, songs by the children (including one written by Fred Summers about LEARN), speeches by several community leaders, and music. The planners of this event had expected a crowd of around 300 and were absolutely astounded when 900 people— mostly parents and community members showed up. This event, where the principal, the superintendent, and other leaders assured parents that things were different, that all stakeholders—especially parents—had an important voice at Jackson, and that they could not and would not move ahead without them, impressed Ramirez tremendously, and slowly she began to attend events at school. Eventually she was asked (we could not determine who did the asking) to be on the site council, a role she happily accepted.

Lena Ramirez, according to Paul, served as a powerful leader during the first years of LEARN implementation in at least two ways. First, she actively supported the work of teachers and served as a link (and sometimes literally a translator) between professional educators and the parents. Second, she encouraged other mothers to become involved. Ramirez herself reports that she was always made to feel welcome at the site council meetings and, for that matter, any time she came on campus. This gave her the courage to become involved as the Little Red Schoolhouse Parent Center was being developed. She was the person who lobbied for English as a Second Language (ESL) classes and was an enthusiastic participant the first time this was offered. And she has continued to remain active in the events held at the center.

Other parents, almost all of them women, seem to be following in Lena Ramirez's footsteps. A core group of approximately eight women attend the Tuesday morning parent meetings regularly, ask questions, and volunteer for various tasks. They reach out to other parents, welcoming newcomers (especially the occasional father who attends) and asking less confident parents to join them as they plan a food sale for the Halloween parade; visit libraries, parks, museums, and the like to see how they could use these to enrich their family's learning; and identify needs and interests of the parents that might mark places where Jackson could connect more fully with its community.

Leading Around Issues of Learning and Teaching

We have not, thus far, observed parents speaking up on instructional issues within the school. However, one recounted to us how she spends time with her cousin, who also has a young child, trying to help her learn to better help her daughter. This mother, Leila Estefan, indicated that she has learned much about good teaching by helping out in her child's classroom. She knows the importance of coaching, of helping children solve problems rather than simply answering their questions, and of encouraging her son to read by listening to him and by providing him with books from Jackson's library. She reports on these learnings to her relative. We were impressed with the fact that Estefan was beginning to develop as an instructional leader, at least within her own family, and we wondered if the same thing might be occurring with other parents.

□ Conclusions

Three points about leadership at Jackson Elementary School seem especially worthy of note. First, the exercise of leadership by the principal and a number of teachers around issues of learning and teaching is, in our estimation, an important factor in this school's success. Second, parents are contributing to the academic success of students by actively and enthusiastically supporting the work of educators. Their leadership can be seen in their work with other parents—not in efforts to influence instruction or school or classroom structures. Third, SBM has had a more direct influence on cultivating leadership among parents. Literally, it has created structures through which they can become involved in governance. Symbolically, it has given them permission—indeed, an invitation—to embrace a more active role in all areas of school life. In the case of administrators and teachers, SBM has provided an environment in which new types of power relations and shared leadership roles can be played out. It has not, in our estimation, created these new relationships and roles. These can be traced to the culture of this school, to the personalities and styles of various individuals, and to events that preceded the onset of shared governance. We have provided evidence in this chapter supporting the three points articulated above, and we will not repeat it here. Rather, in this section, we focus briefly on our assertions that the exercise of leadership by numerous individuals at this site has been shaped to a large extent by Jackson's culture and the fact that SBM has provided a set of opportunities for people to demonstrate their leadership abilities.

Our assertion that Jackson's culture, not its governance structure, the personalities and expectations of various individuals, and events preceding site autonomy are main contributors to shared, fluid, and focused leadership at this site is based on three different types of data. Much comes from our observations of interactions in and around this school. Some comes from self-assessments that were a part of our interview data. Finally, the analysis offered by several veteran teachers of the historical forces that have shaped Jackson's culture and their attitudes and expectations provided important insights.

During our time at Jackson, most of the active attempts on the part of individuals or groups to influence policies or practices at Jackson occurred in the day-to-day life of the school and in faculty meetings. In contrast, the meetings of the site council were fairly relaxed and usually took the form of brainstorming sessions. Participants appeared to be concerned about representing needs and concerns of other stakeholders (especially of the teachers) and about setting priorities for the school. In the meetings we observed, we detected no sense that voting members were lobbying for a particular position.[4] Nor did we hear members suggest that they needed to serve as leaders to convince the rest of the stakeholders. Furthermore, we were not aware when decisions had been made, although participants evidently knew how to interpret the conversations, for subsequent meetings would reveal that certain conversations had been viewed as decisive and others pointed to the need for further discussion.

A brief review of a meeting reported in some detail in Chapter 3 exemplifies this point. This was the meeting at which the allocation of over $100,000 was being discussed. The council members listed a variety of ways to spend this money, and conversation ensued about the instructional benefits of expenditures, about the most pressing needs of teachers, and about the most cost-effective ways to make some improvements to the plant. At times, the coordinator acted as a kind of referee in this discussion, explaining that some monies could be used only in certain ways. The chair for this meeting kept track of this discussion by creating a kind of chart, occasionally linking items by a circle or marking through something that was outside the realm of possibilities. When no one disagreed about an item and everyone seemed enthusiastic, the chair underlined it or drew a star by it. When questions were raised, she placed a question mark beside the notation. No one voted, and there was actually no oral summary at the end of the meeting.

At the next site council meeting, Paul was asked to report on the progress of expenditures. She reported on items that had been ordered and discussed what she had learned about some alternative ways to fund some plant improvements (e.g., "the district will paint two classrooms per year, free of charge"). And she noted that they had decided to wait on the expenditures that someone had questioned.

The casualness of the site council might suggest that people are nonchalant about leadership. This, however, does not appear to be the case. Paul repeatedly discussed her commitment to a form of leadership that assumed that others were equally committed and that, at least in the case of teachers, they were professionals. At least four teachers told of making conscious efforts to serve as leaders. Furthermore, Paul reported that she made deliberate and open efforts to expose teachers to information that would enable them to make what she considered to be "good decisions." However, she also told of consciously and graciously yielding to teachers even when she was unsure about their plans. One teacher with whom we spoke indicated that this was the case and that "[Paul] went to bat for us with the district. She wasn't sure about it, but she trusted us as professionals, and she got permission from them for us to try some new things."

At least four teachers with whom we spoke told of making conscious decisions about serving as leaders even though it meant extra work and extra time commitments. One was the individual who first pushed her colleagues to consider LEARN. Another was a teacher who was passionate about creating a better report card for Jackson's children. Yet another teacher indicated her commitment to working with new teachers, and a fourth spoke about involvement with the union both at this site and in the city and state.

In many schools we have visited, administrators struggle to recruit teachers and parents into decision-making positions. At Jackson, people seem to recognize that they need to respond to the leadership imperative if things are to move in good directions, and they do so in a very fluid manner. At one point, an individual may be guiding a conversation, giving advice, or providing support. Then, a few minutes later, that person will be on the receiving end of a similar sort of interaction. Dispersed leadership of many is a cultural norm at this site.

As we learned more about the history of Jackson, we gained insight into one way such a culture might have evolved. In Chapter 2, we spoke of the history of this school, stressing that the principal before Leah Paul had been quite a disciplinarian. One teacher indicated that this individual's "toughness" was due in part to the nature of the school and community when she took it over. Evidently, Jackson had been a center of gang activity. It had the reputation of being a dangerous school where younger children were adversely affected by the behaviors of older students and gangs who simply used the campus as a hangout. Teachers did not want to teach there, and according to our teacher informant, "many didn't last a year here." She continued by stating,

[Ms. Burns] [the principal preceding Paul] really cleaned up this place. She had to. And she made it clear to us that we had to be tough. There was no nonsense with her. And we got tough. It was the only way to survive. In fact, we became an ornery bunch of teachers. We felt like [Jackson] was ours. We had "taken it back."

This teacher then described the transition to the more relaxed, supportive style of Leah Paul.

I think we might have overwhelmed her at first, but we're learning to work together well. She's not as strong on discipline, but we're good at order and at getting things done. And she treats us like professionals in our classrooms. We make decisions that we couldn't make under [Burns].

Another teacher told a similar story, concurring that teachers who came to Jackson under Principal Burns and stayed there had strong commitments to children and to this school and community. They had worked hard individually and collectively to create a safe, disciplined environment and had developed an esprit de corps and a kind of pride in their resilience long before SBM came to this site. Thus, we contend that the culture of this school—a culture that was shaped by the personalities of various stakeholders and by historical events—and not SBM is the prime shaper of leadership at this site. Furthermore, we argue that the broad-based exercise of leadership, especially around issues of learning and teaching, contributes to the success Jackson is experiencing today.

The words of Leah Paul offered in a lengthy conversation off-site during the summer of 1995 provide a nice summary of these ideas. When asked specifically about the role of governance in Jackson's transformation, she replied,

There's a lot to be said for LEARN, but nothing connected with it guarantees that things will work. We changed quickly when our teachers had a chance to discover and use really effective teaching strategies.

She continued:

When I was with the district, I pulled together a resource bank of information about good teaching approaches. It was all in these huge notebooks with overviews of different approaches and research about them—when they worked, why they were supposed to work, that kind of thing. Of course, when I left, nothing happened to that. But it benefited me, because I had a chance to learn a lot about teaching and the theories and research connected to it.

When I came to [Jackson] and we became a LEARN school, it was like we had permission to rethink everything. As we set our goals, it was natural for us to think about the best ways to reach them. We found some good strategies— like Storyline—and, fortunately, the faculty were able and willing to try them.

I didn't push them, but I was determined to expose them to possibilities. And if they wanted to try something, I was absolutely determined to see that they got all the training they needed to do it well. Fortunately, they did want to use these new strategies. In fact, I can barely hold them back. They've been trained and then they've taken the ideas and made them theirs. It's great when that happens.

□ Notes

1. In a recent article in *Educational Researcher*, Richard Elmore (1995) points out a number of factors that tend to lead reformers to focus on changing structures even though evidence such as that offered by Geraci (1995), Guskey and Peterson (1995), and Murphy and Beck (1995) suggests that structures often do little to contribute to reform.

2. Those schools that did ask for waivers were almost exclusively schools with vocal parents. In a few of these sites, it seemed politic *and* in the spirit of LEARN to have more parents on the governance council.

3. The vast majority of Jackson's students are Roman Catholics and are quite comfortable with traditional or Mexican decorations. However, some of the students and two teachers are Jehovah's Witnesses and do not celebrate any holidays. At least one teacher is a fundamentalist Christian with a strong belief in the importance of

dealing with the realm of the spiritual, and several teachers are Jewish.

4. Principal Leah Paul, although she does not "lobby" for a particular issue, does, by her own admission, work behind the scenes ahead of time to influence the thinking of the council about instructional issues.

5

The Community Imperative

In recent years, calls for "community building" (Sergiovanni, 1994, p. xi) in schools have been issued by a variety of individuals interested in school improvement. These have been inspired by a growing understanding both of the meaning of community and of the value of its cultivation for educational institutions. One group of advocates builds its arguments, at least in part, on analyses of "goodness" in schools offered by Barth (1990); Bryk and Driscoll (1988); Bryk, Lee, and Holland (1993); Lightfoot (1984); Metz (1986); Murphy, Hallinger, and Mesa (1985); Rutter, Maughan, Mortimore, and Ouston (1979); Sergiovanni (1994); and others. Frequently drawing on empirical work that notes correlations among "communal organization" (Bryk et al., 1993, p. 287), "adult commitment," and the realization of "important social and academic benefits . . . to students" (Bryk & Driscoll, 1988, p. 3), these authors suggest that the community plays an important role in promoting satisfaction, engagement, and learning.

A second school of thought emphasizes the value of creating schools that serve as the organizing centers for community-based service agencies working with children and families (e.g., Center for the Future of Children, 1992; Committee for Economic Development, 1987, 1991; Halpern, 1990; Hodgkinson, 1989; Schorr, 1989). Frequently, persons writing in this vein emphasize the political, economic, and educational efficiencies of situating virtually all of the developmental services for children in sites likely to be in contact with the majority of families in a community.

A third group of scholars (Dewey, 1900, 1966; Heckman, Confer, & Peacock, 1995; Herriman, 1995; Schorr, 1989) asserts that schools have a moral imperative to serve as centers of democracy. For these persons, the call for community building is not merely instrumental; it is also a moral imperative. They tend to focus both on the cultivation of community within schools and on linkages between schools and stakeholders outside of the educational arena. Dewey, for example, insists that a primary purpose of schooling is to provide opportunities for the development of productive citizenship. Heckman and his coauthors (1995) and Herriman (1995), in turn, focus on the necessity of allowing citizens affected by the work of schools to have a voice in shaping their goals, activities, and structures.

Yet another group of thinkers offers arguments similar to those of Heckman and his colleagues (1995) and Herriman (1995) but presents radically different rationales for involving the community in the work of schools. These individuals often look to political and economic theories as they assert that community control of schools helps to create tight systems of accountability. It is reasoned that educators, who must answer to representatives of the local community, including parents, will be much more responsive to local interests, needs, and concerns. The community, in turn, will be in a better position to monitor and regulate educational enterprises and personnel (e.g., Boyd & O'Shea, 1975; Chubb & Moe, 1990; La Noue & Smith, 1973; Lewis, 1993; Rogers, 1981).

As we have reported elsewhere (Murphy & Beck, 1995), advocates of site-based management (SBM) can be located within each of these schools of thought. Some insist that autonomy from centralized control creates a number of conditions that encourage a more communal school organization (e.g., Bryk et al., 1993). Others point out that schools are more able to create positive and collaborative relationships with community organizations if "the role of district and state administrators" shifts "from rule making and monitoring" to supporting local initiatives (e.g., Jehl & Kirst, 1992). Many proponents of SBM argue that this form of governance allows parents and the community to have a voice in greater educational decision making (e.g., Lewis, 1993; Wohlstetter & Smyer, 1994). And a number assert that accountability to the community is enhanced when control of schools is localized (e.g., Bimber, 1993). As we noted earlier, in the logic of SBM, local autonomy creates conditions under which curriculum, teaching strategies, budgeting practices, schedules, decision-making structures, and the like will lead to student achievement and adult satisfaction (Bryk, 1993; Mojkowski & Fleming, 1988).

As a part of our investigation at Jackson, we sought to assess the degree to which this part of the causal logic of site autonomy matched this school's reality. To do this, we first sought to understand the ways persons at this site understood and cultivated community. We then untangled, as much as possible, the interactions between community, governance structure, and manifestations of success at this site. Thus, we analyzed our data to (a) uncover the meanings of "community" that seemed to shape the thinking and practice of Jackson's stakeholders, (b) consider the ways in which community, in the form(s) it took, contributed to, or was influenced by, the various successes of this site and (c) tease apart the interactions between responses to the community imperative, other forces driving work at this school, and Jackson's decision-making structures. For the balance of this chapter, we use these three foci as an organizing scheme.

□ The Meaning of Community at Jackson Elementary School

Early on, when we began to engage in informal conversations about the things we were seeing and hearing at Jackson, one word—*family*—recurred frequently. This was a metaphor that captured for us many things about this site. Often it seemed to us that site council decision-making sessions in their content and processes were like those families might have, with persons sitting somewhat haphazardly around (and even on) tables, engaging in easy and candid conversation in the absence of formal "Robert's Rules of Order"-type procedures. Interactions between teachers—especially those between veterans and novices—seemed so natural that they too caused us to think of the help siblings or parents and children might offer to each other. We even began to feel, in a certain sense, like we were a part of the family there. Never was this more evident than the day that several big events were occurring, including a Storyline culmination and a holiday assembly. One of us arrived this day, camera in hand, and felt a genuine measure of pride (and a bit of parentlike anxiety) as she watched the children and received hugs from some of the excited participants as their programs ended.

Interestingly, as we analyzed our data, we discovered that we were not the only ones likening Jackson School to a family. The metaphor and a number of related themes frequently appeared in conversations we had or overheard. As we analyzed not only the words but also the events we observed, two themes emerged time and again that helped us understand how to characterize Jackson's understanding of community. The first of these relates to the embeddedness of a sense of family that was apparently shared by most teachers, administrators, and staff. The assumption that working at this school meant that one belonged and that she or he would be accepted and cared for and would, in turn, care for others was widespread here. The second theme relates to the way an understanding of education's academic purposes was repeatedly framed as honoring a commitment to children and families of Jackson's local community.

Functioning as a Family-Like Community

Although parents and administrators likened Jackson Elementary School to a family, it was the teachers who were most articulate in using this metaphor. Most often they spoke in glowing terms of other teachers and of a profound sense of mutual care; however, they also included administrators in their discussions, noting that care from them often took the form of clear expressions of trust in, and support of, personal and professional judgment. Several also made the point that classified staff were also regarded as respected members of the Jackson family who were treated as colleagues in most social and professional development activities, and at least five teachers spoke of a personal and conscious commitment to expand their understanding of community to include parents. Furthermore, with only one exception,[1] the teachers we interviewed cited the quality of collegial relationships and friendships among adults and the sense of family at Jackson as important contributors to their ability to work creatively and effectively with students.

We were impressed by the pervasiveness of the view that people at this site possessed something approaching an unconditional regard for one another. Over and over, people would acknowledge disagreements or preferences for some personalities over others, but they would immediately say that these did not affect the mutual commitment and support here. Indeed, teachers, virtually to the person, spoke at length about the quality of relationships here and about the profound care that was both received and given. And several gave examples of ways care was offered to them simply because they were part of this community, and these persons saw this as a distinguishing feature of Jackson Elementary School.

One teacher, when asked about factors that caused her to stay at Jackson for 7 years, answered immediately, "It's—the people are very, the people are more—it's the staff. When you go to other schools and visit, you can see the segregation [between groups of teachers and teachers and staff]. We tend to, we socially all get along." Her subsequent words, however, revealed that their interactions went well beyond "getting along." She noted, for example, that high levels of personal and professional caring were accorded to new teachers before they were well-known and had "proven themselves," as well as to those who had established themselves.

> [Jackson] is . . . the best place in the world for a new teacher to start out. Everybody shares. Everybody has a box full of whatever unit somebody wants to start on, that encompasses every subject in it. It's real sharing and helpful in that way. So it's a great place for anybody who's beginning. It's also a good place for people with experience . . . it's cohesive. Some of my best friends [are here].

This teacher went on to talk at length about the depth and quality of friendships at this site. Beginning with a reminder that many faculty members had young children ("I think we have like 23 kids"), she laughingly stated, "We all kind of ride through the pregnancies and all that kind of junk together" and noted that even the older teachers and the single men join in.

Like [Ann Jones] is real good on mom advice. She's dying to have a grandchild, so she's been a real support for all of us going through it. . . . And some of the men teachers on staff . . . [her daughter] has been adopted by [Tim Stein] as an uncle. So they also fit in and become part of the group. And we're supportive of each other. People have gone through things like losses in the family and stuff. And we do manage to get out of here and go to the funerals and help support the kind of things they go through and be there for one another.

Another teacher, only 2 years at this site, told similar stories about high levels of professional care and support from colleagues.

If you're going to be working on something, all you have to do is say, "I'm working on such and such," and you're going to have people who are going to volunteer materials, help. [Karen Doss] walked in here the other day and said, "Oh, you're doing Africa. I have a bunch of Kwanza posters and things. I'll bring them by to you." I didn't even have to ask. She just looked and saw and said, "I'll help."

Her stories also confirmed that personal caring was extended to her from her first day on site.

As far as on a personal level, when my husband went through treatment for cancer last year, he was diagnosed— let's see. He went to the doctor and received his diagnosis the day I was setting up my classroom for the first day of school here, and so that's how I started out the year last year. And they were very, very concerned on a personal level— very caring. . . . When he went into the hospital, I had teachers who showed up with dinner for my family. They said, "You don't need to go home and try and worry about cooking for your kids. You need to be at the hospital." And they offered to come in and cover my class for the last half hour of school so I could leave early and beat traffic down to LA, to the hospital. That was [Sandra Brown]. She said, "I don't have any kids the last half hour today. Why don't I come in and . . ." So there are some very caring, very concerned

people that are really pulling together, not just on a professional level as far as making their classes what they should
be but helping each other, and that was really neat to me. And
as far as when he went in for surgery and things. [Leah
Paul's] attitude was, "You take as many days as you need."

This teacher and others reported that in their view, supportive
relationships among faculty, staff, and administrators positively influenced their work with children in a variety of ways. Several spoke
of the fact that they happily and freely gave of personal time to
improve teaching and spent their own money to buy supplies because of this strong sense of connection to one another and to the
school. For instance, one noted, "I mean, when I spend $150 bucks
on posters, that's my $150 bucks, and I don't mind at all because to
me this is where I work, and I get so much out of it! It pumps me up
when I look at this stuff." One teacher noted that the teaching
assistants, who are often community members, are viewed as wonderful partners in the classroom, and she suggested that part of their
ability to work so effectively related to their inclusion in professional
development activities. "They get trained in new ways of teaching
just like we do. So they're really able to help us and the kids." Another
indicated that the sense that administrators and teaching colleagues
trusted and respected her gave her confidence to "go out of the circle
[and] do what [she] need[ed] to do to teach these kids to learn to
read." She felt that she could share both her successes and failures
with colleagues and that they would learn with her about better ways
to work with youngsters.

Several teachers acknowledged that this sense of family that was
so widespread and powerful among educators at this site had only
recently begun to extend to parents and others in the larger community. They, however, were open about their efforts to expand their
circle of concern and support. At least three things seemed to be
shaping their thinking in this way. One was the establishment of the
Little Red Schoolhouse as a Parent Center. At least two teachers noted
that they wanted to get to know family members, but they felt
"swamped" by large classes and the many demands on their time.
They indicated, however, that having a structure that offered classes
for parents and family-oriented academic activities was assisting
them in getting to know parents and was helping the parents in
understanding the teachers and the school.

A second factor credited by teachers and administrators for building bridges between teachers and parents was the adoption of more constructivist teaching strategies—especially Scottish Storyline. Fred Summers was one who explained this phenomenon. He reported that prior to Storyline, his teaching had been shaped by his way of understanding the world. "I would create themes and draw links between things, but it was my logic that was shaping what I did. It made sense to me, but I'm not sure the kids saw it." As he began to implement Scottish Storyline in his classes and to involve the students more actively in problem solving, he found that they were drawing on their own knowledge and culture. To his surprise, he began to learn more about his students and their families, and he came to respect all that they brought to the learning enterprise. Furthermore, he began to draw parents into his class—both as resources and as participants. Leah Paul reported that new ways of teaching were having a similar effect on other teachers. She noted that the teachers "decided to abandon the yearly parent-teacher night," opting instead to bring parents in for every Storyline culmination. "When they're here and see our classes and what we're doing, they learn about being partners with us. And we begin to involve them also."

A third factor that seemed to be influencing greater parental and community involvement at this site was the example of Leah Paul and other administrators as they actively reached out to involve parents substantively in decision making and planning. Always in attendance at the weekly parent meetings held in the Little Red Schoolhouse were at least three members of the administrative team. These individuals participated in these meetings, but they never—while we were there—in any way dominated them. Rather, they provided information and often acted as liaisons between parents and school or district officials or policies. In the first role, they might steer parents expressing concerns about health or parenting to appropriate resources in the community. In the latter, they would do things such as assisting parents in scheduling and finding teachers for the various classes offered through the Little Red Schoolhouse.

Even more important, Jackson's administrators apparently were quite consistent in making extra efforts to invite and welcome parents at governance meetings and to include them when important decisions were being made. For example, when Leah Paul and lead teacher Mary Graves were invited to attend a meeting with state superintendent Delaine Eastin to discuss reform initiatives in Los Angeles, they specifically invited a parent to join them, introduced her to everyone, and ensured that she was included in conversations.

These efforts of the administration were recognized and appreciated by parents with whom we spoke. One woman, Marita Ramirez, told us about attending meetings with Leah Paul and others. When asked if she felt that others listened to her as a parent, she replied, "Yes, I do, they listen to me." Then she added, "Also, when I go there, they go, 'Oh [Marita], welcome.' Otherwise, I would feel very bad. Standing there, I can feel—you can feel when somebody doesn't pay attention to you." Another parent, currently holding a part-time position as community liaison at Jackson, when asked how the administration supported her, responded with these words:

> Well, I feel a lot of support. Um, they trust me. They always invite me to participate in all the activities. They respect my opinions. . . . And they believe in me. And that's something that's mainly—that's why I'm here—because I feel comfortable. I feel trusted.

Unlike the teachers, parents did not as readily or naturally view Jackson as a family. However, the four parents with whom we spoke were unanimous in indicating that in recent years they have grown increasingly comfortable as a part of this community. Each also provided us with examples of times when they had spoken up in meetings with teachers and administrators or both and reported that each time they did this their confidence and sense of belonging increased.

Understanding Jackson's Purpose as Promoting Learning for the Children of This Local Community

Although teachers were quite vocal about the value they placed on the quality of relationships at this site, they were equally clear that the centerpiece of these was their wholesale commitment to "their" children. Furthermore, a number pointed out that for them, this commitment was honored especially in the academic arena as they sought to promote excellent learning for students.

One teacher who stated, "I stay here because the people I work with are so supportive and creative" was clear that underlying and inspiring relationships among adults was a commitment to "helping as many people and as many children as possible learn as much as possible and in the process making it a vibrant creative experience." Another teacher, who had spoken at some length of the meaningful and supportive relationships among teachers, was careful to stress that adult friendships did not distract them from their goals to prepare students "in every way we can possibly prepare them—academically . . . [and] as far as an educational mind-set is concerned." One teacher used slightly different words when she described the foundation of Jackson's culture with these words: "We empower our children. That's the word. [Jackson's] staff tries to empower students."

The teacher who spoke of empowerment, a 10-year veteran at Jackson, was quite articulate about the fact that this school was strongly committed to the local neighborhood and its residents. Indeed, she referred by name to a former student who sometimes assisted the teachers and stated,

> Watching him as a man now makes me feel pretty old, but he comes in here, and he looks at these guys, and it's the same. . . . It makes me feel really special because he recognizes as a man that the things we did at [Jackson] got him to where he is now. He's a college student. He has returned to his neighborhood and to his school. And that's powerful— that's very powerful when you have people come back to be where they started. And he's not the only one. Constantly, I get high school kids that I've taught. They all want to come back here and teach. They want to do it. And that's [Jackson]. . . . We're very free-spirited here, and we don't put on airs for anybody. And this is [Jackson]. There are a lot of things we'd like to do that we don't do because time doesn't permit it, but we're dedicated, and we love our youngsters. That's [Jackson].

For this teacher, the commitment to student learning and to the youngsters of this local community went hand in hand.

Another example of the commitment of Jackson's staff to promote the achievement of individuals within their local community can be seen in the collaborations between this school and others in this part of the city. As we noted in Chapter 2, Jackson is one of several elementary schools that serves a low-income area of Los Angeles. Although there is some transiency in this community, a fair number of residents locate here for some length of time, and many children move out of an elementary school into one of two middle schools. Virtually all of them then attend the single high school that serves this part of the city. Most of these schools have elected to become LEARN schools and have thus received some autonomy from the district. Interestingly, the principals and teachers from these institutions who were attending the training sessions for LEARN school leaders began to consider the value of voluntarily aligning themselves with one another, sharing expertise and resources. They began a process of collaboration that is, according to one school board member, "unprecedented in this city's history." The quality of Jackson's participation in this collaboration provides additional insight into the nature of its commitment to the children of this neighborhood.

Within this group of schools, Jackson has been the one to adopt and implement several innovative and effective pedagogies. Especially for this, it has been recognized as a leader in reform efforts in Los Angeles. Jackson is frequently chosen for visits by policymakers and funders and is often mentioned by name by Mike Roos, the president of LEARN, as an exemplary site. Furthermore, this school has been featured in a multipage, color spread in a local newspaper (Kindy, 1995), and Leah Paul and Jackson's teachers are frequent presenters at local and area conferences. Also, Jackson was identified by name in an evaluation of the LEARN reform efforts as one of three schools in the city that had shown remarkable improvement in the past few years (McKinsey & Co, 1994).

We rarely heard teachers or administrators mention any of this acclaim during our months at this site. We did, however, hear Leah Paul and the teachers speak on several occasions of sharing ideas and knowledge with other schools in the community. Furthermore, we witnessed a number of interactions during which educators from this site openly assisted their colleagues in partner institutions who were seeking to institute innovations.

Even more impressive than the sharing of knowledge, however, was the collaborative use of financial resources and personnel among schools in this attendance area. Leah Paul and other principals in this neighborhood, supported apparently by the leadership teams of their respective schools, had regular meetings in which they considered ways they might work together: writing grants, sharing resources, connecting with health and other social services, hiring individuals collaboratively, and the like. The guiding theme of these meetings was, in the words of one teacher, "our commitment to improve the achievement of every child, prekindergarten through twelfth grade, in this community." Jackson's commitment to the larger community was, in our estimation, demonstrated by its work with other schools on activities even when no specific or immediate benefit to the site was obvious.

☐ **Responses to the Community Imperative and Jackson's Success**

The Development of a Sense of Community at Jackson

Our best clues to the links between the strong sense of community at Jackson and the success we witnessed came from conversations with teachers, especially with those who had been at this site for some time. Both those who were somewhat critical of the principal who had preceded Leah Paul and the many who spoke fondly of her credited Sharon Burns with doing much to build a sense of esprit de corps at Jackson. Although teachers had different reactions to the rigidity of this administrator and to the structures she imposed and policies she enforced, most agreed that these had a unifying effect on the faculty. Three teachers, independently of one another, suggested that this could be explained, in part, by the process by which teachers entered into this community. They recalled that Burns had a rigorous method of interviewing teachers that included having applicants spend a full day on site. One commented that "not only were they getting an idea of the things we did and how we did them, [but] we were getting a feel for them and how they would fit in." Another noted that people were offered jobs at Jackson if it was apparent that they would fit in and contribute.

The talents that we were chosen for, like anyplace, you know, it's like a bonfire. You pick the right kind of wood because you want to have a good fire. Well, she [the former principal] picked the right kind of wood.

Two other teachers offered a different perspective on the ways the style of the previous principal helped to create a strong and supportive community. Both of them suggested that teachers pulled together and became friends for support when the administration was difficult. Regardless of their views, teachers agreed that the sense of family at this site predated the instructional changes that seemed to be so central to Jackson's present-day success.

Furthermore, each of the five teachers who contributed insights into the impact of Susan Burns on the sense of family at Jackson indicated that they believed that this spirit of community made making instructional changes easier for them. None, however, credited it with being the central force propelling change. Two grounded both the caring, supportive ethos and the willingness to take risks and to try new things in Jackson's culture. One, who labeled her colleagues as being "creative and supportive," summed up her views and those of her colleagues when she described Jackson's culture this way:

We're innovative . . . we're forerunners. . . . We're not afraid to try new things and pilot new programs and experiments 'cause we're always looking for what's the best thing for kids.

Two others who, not coincidentally, were the ones who were not especially fond of the previous principal, gave much credit for the innovations to Leah Paul's leadership and trust in them as professionals and suggested that the strong sense of support and community hastened the ability of teachers to embrace and implement exciting pedagogies. And virtually every teacher, both veterans and those new to the site, reported their impression that the supportive sense of community—especially the helpfulness and willingness to share among teachers—escalated the speed by which new curricular and instructional strategies were successfully adapted and institutionalized. At this site, the sharing of ideas about teaching seemed to have immediate benefits in that individuals were quick to appropriate in their classes things they learned from colleagues often with obvious, and at times dramatic, success.

SBM, the Community Imperative, and Success

A number of teachers with whom we spoke believed that SBM benefited the school in several ways. They did not, however, credit local autonomy with creating a sense of community among them. Indeed, the words of many suggested that it was the other way around—that the spirit of community enabled SBM to work as well as it did. One suggested that the school as a whole, and the site council specifically, were able to work through disagreements and to reach consensus fairly quickly because they trusted each other, practiced give-and-take on issues, and knew how to interact effectively.

> You have to be cooperative. You have to be compromising, you know. . . . Sometimes it's your way and sometimes it's my way, and sometimes it's a different way that neither one of us is happy with, but we'll work together on it.

Leah Paul, interestingly enough, indicated that she felt that in many instances the sense of community almost made the need for formal governance obsolete.

> There's a lot of trust. It's not like everything needs to be hashed out all the time. We don't have to mark our territory at every meeting. There are a lot of assumptions about why we're here and what we're about that make us able to reach agreement fairly easily.

Our observations at council meetings and faculty meetings coupled with our analysis of documents from this site confirmed, in general, Paul's impressions that community in many ways both superseded and supported local governance. Many fundamental issues that frequently are sources of contention, such as the composition of the governing body or the specific processes of decision making, were apparently almost nonissues here. Conspicuous by their absence from meetings—and indeed, from conversations of faculty, staff, and parents—were discussions of rights or representation. Even when tense issues were dealt with (such as the reconfiguring of all elementary schools away from a K-6 grade scheme to a K-5 format to create middle schools), teachers expressed no apprehension in meetings or in conversations with us that they would be treated unfairly by Jackson's administration. In fact, several suggested that they trusted Leah Paul "to get the best deal possible" for them from the district.

□ **Conclusions**

Responses to the community imperative at Jackson Elementary School seemed to go beyond action items, processes, and procedures and to be nested in the ways teachers, administrators, staff, and a few parents thought about themselves and their work. People appeared to be bound together both by a strong concern about student learning and by commitments to and friendships with one another.

We could not find evidence that SBM contributed much to either the academic vision or the communal ethos at Jackson as it extended to educators. We did, however, learn from several parents that they felt that they were more a part of the school as a result of LEARN. Symbolically, the open and ongoing invitation to join in governance combined with the presence of structures such as the site council and the Little Red Schoolhouse. These efforts provided parents with a sense that they were welcome and important and resulted in more involvement and a stronger sense of ownership from this group of stakeholders.

The advent of SBM at Jackson and in other schools in this neighborhood had also created opportunities for collaboration among these institutions to benefit all the children of this geographic community. This working together across sites did not emanate from the fact that sites were more autonomous. It was, however, made possible because individual schools had a measure of freedom from the district in the areas of staff development and resource use. The schools of this community sought to coordinate their staff development to increase the smoothness of articulation between grades and schools and to provide students with a more coherent, quality educational experience, and on several occasions, they creatively shared resources and personnel across sites. Paul (and, for that matter, other principals and teachers in this complex of schools) believed that they were more able to make effective linkages with each other and with the community because they were not burdened with so many district constraints.

At Jackson Elementary School, the strong sense of community among the staff predated and contributed to both the effectiveness of SBM and the school's successful embrace of instructional strategies. On the other hand, local autonomy and the particular governance structures that accompanied being a LEARN school seemed to be a stronger force in the bringing of parents on site and into activities at Jackson. Freedom from some mandates and constraints in the highly bureaucratized Los Angeles Unified School District also helped to create conditions that enabled Jackson to join with other schools in its neighborhood to develop strategies for working more effectively with all the children in this community.

☐ Note

1. The only teacher who did not volunteer information about her friendships at this site was one who had been at Jackson for less than a month. She did talk about what appeared to her to be a positive atmosphere, but she did not feel that she had been at this site long enough to establish relationships.

6

The Capacity-Building Imperative

Site-based management (SBM) assumes, among other things, that decisions made by individuals within a local community will in all likelihood be better than those made by persons removed from a specific setting. The presumption is that teachers, administrators, and parents, armed with knowledge of specific locales and with high levels of self-interest, will seek out and implement curricula and pedagogies likely to promote high levels of learning, efficient use of resources, and the like.

As we note in Chapter 1 and elsewhere (Murphy & Beck, 1995), very little evidence supports the validity of this assumption. Even in sites where researchers report high levels of stakeholder involvement in decision making and often great satisfaction with this reality, few changes in learning and teaching are evident (e.g., Easton, 1991; Fullan, 1993; Taylor & Teddlie, 1992; Weiss, 1992). Several researchers (e.g., Daresh, 1992; Duttweiler & Mutchler, 1990; Murphy, 1991; Murphy & Hallinger, 1993) have suggested that this may be due in part to "resource liabilities" (Malen & Ogawa, 1988, p. 263) especially in the areas of time (Bachus, 1991; Brown, 1990; Carnoy & MacDonnell, 1990; Chapman, 1990; Collins & Hanson, 1991), management skills (Mutchler & Duttweiller, 1990), and knowledge of effective instructional strategies (Fullan, 1993).

In previous chapters, we have alluded to ways in which planning and resources at Jackson Elementary School have been used to provide time, skills, and knowledge to this site's stakeholders. Here we explore this phenomenon in greater detail as we seek to understand (a) the nature of capacity-building efforts at this site, (b) how such efforts have contributed to successful reform, and (c) interactions between focused professional and parental development efforts and SBM. In the following sections, we discuss each of these topics.

□ **The Breadth and Depth of Capacity-Building Efforts at Jackson**

Conversations with Leah Paul and other administrators, teachers, staff, and parents, coupled with observations at this site, indicated that developing the abilities of adults to work effectively together and with children is a top priority at Jackson. We have already alluded to many of the efforts that reflect this priority: the development of the Little Red Schoolhouse with a host of classes for parents, the scheduling of collaborative planning time for teachers, the provision of a coherent set of in-house professional development activities, and the support and encouragement of teachers' receiving off-site additional training in new pedagogical strategies. Rather than focusing on any one of these in detail, in this section, we provide an overview of the various capacity-building efforts in an effort to (a) demonstrate both the breadth and depth of such activities and (b) underscore the fact that professional development at this site is guided primarily by the widespread commitment to respond to the learning imperative.

Our first contact with teachers and administrators at Jackson Elementary School was in a professional development setting. As noted earlier, we met principal Leah Paul and lead teacher Mary Graves in 1993 during an intensive, 5-week summer institute for LEARN school leaders. This training experience included a number of "Stakeholder Days" during which parents, classified staff members, and teachers were invited to join the two educators attending the institute to begin collaborative planning for the larger school community. For some LEARN schools, identifying people willing to participate in these development activities and making arrangements for them to do so were quite a challenge. This was not the case for Jackson. From the beginning, Paul, Graves, the assistant principal, and the coordinator worked together to ensure that parents were fully informed and included and that personnel were hired to cover the work of teachers and classified staff so that they could attend these training days. In the months we spent at Jackson, we learned that the administrative support of capacity building for all stakeholders that we witnessed in our early contact with this school was quite typical. Furthermore, we discovered that administrators, teachers, and a growing group of parents were enthusiastic "consumers" of development opportunities.

Capacity-building efforts at this site focused on three things. Many revolved around equipping teachers with knowledge and skills to support student learning. Others were aimed at assisting parents in developing skills that would ultimately enhance their abilities to help their children in and out of school. A smaller number of professional development activities focused on developing the skills of administrators, teachers, and parents so that they would be able to address the challenges associated with SBM. Many of the efforts consisted of formal training sessions that required the allocation of financial resources and time. Others were less structured and involved setting aside regular periods of time for teachers to encourage collaboration and the sharing of knowledge and ideas.

Capacity Building and Teachers

During the months we were at Jackson, we observed teachers' participating in a host of professional development activities. We learned of others in conversations and through documents recounting the school's recent history. The majority of these were structured training activities designed to assist teachers in understanding and implementing new teaching strategies.

We have discussed Scottish Storyline training in previous chapters. Here we just reiterate some key features of this professional development activity that are typical of Jackson Elementary School.

The decision to use Storyline at Jackson was made by teachers with the encouragement and support of Leah Paul and lead teacher Mary Graves. Once this occurred, two things happened. Paul told teachers interested in learning this pedagogy that they would "find a way to get training" for them, and Elise May, a teacher and academic coordinator, wrote a grant proposal to the State Department of Education, seeking funds to cover the cost of such training. According to Paul, she invited teachers to participate without knowing how many would respond or exactly how they would find the monies to cover expenses.[1] However, she "felt that this was a key investment." Indeed, recalling her attitude at the time, she stated, "It never occurred to me that we wouldn't find a way to do this. I never had a doubt."

To Paul's surprise, approximately 20 teachers (of a staff of 39) asked for Storyline training. Paul and May made arrangements for all of these to attend a 5-day workshop, hiring substitutes to cover classes that would be missed. This involved making a commitment to spend over $6,000 for this single activity.[2] Reflecting on the plan for such a large allocation of resources for one project, Paul suggested that several things about it had a powerful impact on the faculty. She noted that the quick "turnaround time" between the teachers' decision to embrace Storyline and the actual provision of training was an important morale booster.

> Here we had become a LEARN school and there was all this talk about self-determination. It was important that that became real for teachers. We didn't even have the budget from the district when we decided to go with this, but we needed to go ahead. I figured that we could do this even if it was our only inservice. Fortunately, we were able to do more, but we had to do this.

Paul also expressed her belief that the investment of time and money to provide in-depth training was symbolically and substantively important.

> There's nothing more important than excellent professional development. That's something we seem to miss in this

district. We've got so many inservice, one-shot programs that basically do nothing but take up teachers' time. I knew we'd never make changes without serious, substantive training in the best teaching out there.

Because Jackson received a grant for $20,000 to support Storyline training, the LEARN council readily agreed that the school could and should support additional learning activities for teachers. In every case, teachers decided on those they wanted to pursue. However, as noted, Paul was quite adept at orchestrating things so that they were exposed to approaches she believed would be beneficial. According to our calculations, since 1993 every teacher has received professional development, in addition to Storyline training, in some method of enhancing students' literacy skills; and six teachers and two administrators have been involved in a course to enable them to use Reading Recovery with children having difficulty in reading. Mentor teachers have been trained in new approaches to mathematics instruction and are now assisting their colleagues in this area, and at least five teachers have received Advanced Storyline training with others requesting this. Several also told us that they were seeking out additional work in a specific area of interest. All of this is in addition to activities offered during the staff development days that are built into the school district's schedule and are a part of every school's calendar.

Teachers' comments indicated that Paul's notion that good professional development had an impact on morale was quite accurate. They also corroborated her idea that the substantive nature of most of the training contributed to improved teaching and enhanced learning. Indeed, the words of one teacher sum up the attitude of many in regard to the impact of support and professional development at this site:

They're [the administration] very attentive to the needs of the school, to the needs of the teacher. They try and do their best. . . . They say, "Well, you do whatever you have to do, set it up, break it down, do the framework, and then present it to us, and we'll work with you, and we'll try and get whatever and as much as you need."

Capacity Building and Parents

Capacity-building efforts for parents, like those for teachers, were directed, in large measure, by the needs and concerns identified by individuals during the weekly meetings at the Little Red School- house. In Chapter 2, we described the first parent meeting we at- tended. At this meeting, participants articulated the areas of great- est concern to them and requested classes related to parenting skills, health and first aid, English language development, computer skills, effective communication, and the like. We were interested to see that administrators, including Jackson's counselor, Lynn Raz, working with Maria Arryas, a parent liaison from the district, and Elise May, the coordinator, arranged to offer every one of these classes at some point during the year. Pulling this off demanded a fair amount of effort from these three individuals, for they had to coor- dinate with a range of agencies and individuals—the adult school located at a nearby high school, the local Red Cross, individuals within the community, and Jackson's administrators and custodial staff—to ensure that qualified instructors had appropriate rooms in which to teach; that they had materials, audiovisual equipment, and translators; and that child care arrangements had been made. These activities, however, apparently did not require separate budget allo- cations. Parenting, ESL, and CPR classes were provided either by the school district or by the Red Cross as a part of their regular program of services. Similarly, translators employed by the district or parents helped to link English-speaking instructors with parents whose pri- mary language was English. Rooms and instructional and audiovisual materials were provided by the school, and frequently older children were enlisted to work with a parent to provide child care during these classes.

Parents appeared to take advantage of the opportunities that were offered to them. Elise May reported that virtually every parent class was well attended with most operating at full capacity. She, Maria Arryas, and five parents with whom we spoke also confirmed comments by Paul and a news article by Kindy (1995) that indicated that parent attendance at school events has increased markedly since 1993 and that the number of parents at the weekly parent meetings had doubled in the past year. We were struck by the fact that during the months we were at Jackson, the number of parents at the meetings we observed climbed steadily. The first ones we attended typically had 25 to 30 mothers present. At the end of our observations, however, we counted between 35 and 40 parents at these events and noted that 4 fathers had joined the group.

Other Capacity-Building Activities

We began our discussion of attitudes toward professional development at Jackson by referring to the training provided to principals and lead teachers by UCLA's School Management Program. This actually consisted of a set of activities aimed at equipping leadership in LEARN schools to handle the tasks that attend SBM. The intensive portion of this program extended for a 15-month period and included training in budgeting as well as technology and opportunities for school leaders to learn strategies for analyzing and influencing their institution's culture. According to Leah Paul and Mary Graves, several aspects of the management program were invaluable to them and affected the way they worked with colleagues at their site.[3]

Graves spoke about the value to her of learning strategies for reshaping an organization. She noted,

Teachers often don't understand the big picture of reform. We see needs or have ideas, but we don't always realize all it takes to pull them off. It was really helpful for me to work with principals and people from the district. It gave me a new sense of all it takes to bring about change. And it was nice to be doing it in an atmosphere where we were all trying to figure out how to make things better.

Paul, in turn, stressed that the training in technology "opened a whole new world" for her:

You know, I never used computers before AMP [Advanced Management Program, the dimension of the School Management Program for LEARN school leaders]. Now I take my powerbook everywhere. It's changed my life. I can stay connected with the school when I'm not there and with the district. It's unbelievable the amount of time I save.

She also noted that decisions by faculty and the LEARN council to bring computers to their site and to provide training in their use for teachers, parents, and students were probably influenced by the training she and Graves received:

> We learned what computers can do. Everyone should learn to use them, but it's especially important for our kids. And the school has to help them. Our families don't have them at home, and yet parents and their children have to be masters of technology if they're going to make it in the "new world."

Both Paul and Graves also spoke at length of another benefit of the training they received. In Graves's words, "This was the first time principals and teachers have sat down together to learn from and with each other. It really helped us understand that making LEARN work means we've got to relate differently." Paul echoed this sentiment and stressed that in her view, it was critical that during the training sessions, principals and teachers were never separated and given different types of information.

> Everything was transparent. When we got our school budgets to work with, we both got them. There was no sense that principals knew something that teachers didn't know. We both learned all of the tricks of working with and around the district. We struggled together over things at our site. [Mary] and I had a good relationship, and because I was new at [Jackson], we didn't have a history of distrust, so it probably didn't affect us as much. But this was really powerful for some other schools.

☐ Capacity Building and School Success

The teachers with whom we spoke at Jackson were outspoken about the value of professional development. They stressed that their success, thus far, in implementing new and successful pedagogies was due, in large measure, to excellent training in these teaching strategies. And they insisted that their ongoing effectiveness would require continuing opportunities to broaden and deepen their professional knowledge and skills.

We have already spoken of teachers' praise of the sense of community at Jackson and of their perception that the supportive relationships they enjoyed with one another and with administrators were an important influence on their behaviors in their classrooms. We stress again that this relational support was not solely social. According to teachers, it was frequently manifested in substantive sharing of knowledge among educators and in the provision of formal opportunities for professional development. Indeed, nine teachers spoke explicitly about the value of participating with their colleagues in high-quality training activities related to implementing Storyline, new strategies for teaching mathematics, or Reading Recovery. One described these shared development activities as having a "reinforcing effect upon all we do." She continued,

> When we participate as a school, we're more able to coach each other and to hold each other accountable and to take risks. Especially when we're doing things that are so different from what we've done. I can't imagine learning Storyline by myself and then having the nerve to turn my room into Antarctica. Even now, it's sometimes tempting to go back to the old "tried-and-true" ways because they're "safe." I know I would have reverted if the others hadn't been there with me.

Others echoed this idea. In fact, every teacher, without exception, commented on the value of learning from colleagues. Two noted that the allocation of an hour each week for collaborative planning was a valuable investment of time and much appreciated by the faculty.

Our observations revealed the fact that teachers' verbal affirmations of the importance of opportunities for professional growth were supported by their behaviors in classrooms. We have described in some detail the widespread implementation of Storyline and the advent of Reading Recovery strategies for students in kindergarten and first grade struggling with reading. We also observed a masterful math lesson by Virginia Peters, a teacher who had been trained in FATHOM, and we learned from her that she is currently working with six other teachers to assist them in learning constructivist "hands-on" math instruction strategies.

As noted earlier, we also observed several scheduled, in-house learning opportunities such as collaborative planning meetings and lunches with mentor teachers each week. Attendance at these was voluntary although there were expectations that all teachers at a particular level would attend and participate in the planning meetings. Regardless, in each get-together we observed at least 6 and sometimes as many as 10 teachers gathered to share ideas or to learn from an experienced educator. A few individuals were quiet at the planning meetings, but most teachers participated. At each meeting, teachers talked about pedagogy, assessment, and curriculum or all three, and they frequently made reference to a recent professional development activity in which they had learned something new. On several occasions, we observed an individual implementing an idea that had been shared by another teacher. This suggested to us that at this site, capacity-building activities at times had a ripple effect, with the learning of one educator influencing the practice of others.

Teachers were not the only ones to demonstrate that development activities were positively affecting the school. We met at least three parents who told us that they were able to converse in English with their children and "to help them learn English quicker" because they had attended ESL classes. And one parent, Marita Ramirez, reported that she never would have joined the LEARN council if she had not become more fluent in English.

They always translate everything, but it's not the same as understanding English. It's really helped me feel better about being there. I can understand what is being said, and sometimes I even talk myself.

Another parent indicated that she believed Jackson was a "really good school" because "teachers are always learning how to help our children."

☐ SBM and the Capacity-Building Imperative

In our earlier discussions of the interactions between SBM and Jackson's response to some imperative, we have pointed out that we are not presenting definitive cause-and-effect evidence. Rather, we are trying to untangle rather complex interactions between governance and reform-oriented activities at this site. This is also the case in our analysis of the links between governance and Jackson's response to the capacity-building imperative. As we sought to understand how the relative autonomy and shared decision making shaped and was shaped by capacity-building activities, we depended primarily on recollections and perceptions of informants. We also drew on our observations of meetings in which professional development was planned, discussed, and arranged.

After analyzing data from these sources, we have concluded that SBM at Jackson *legitimized* involving stakeholders in choosing their development pathways. We are not, however, convinced that it *caused* this participatory decision making. We saw nothing in teacher and parent deliberations that could not occur at most sites—even those under a more centralized governance structure. We did, however, detect a sense of agency on the part of Jackson's stakeholders. They believed that decisions they made about desirable development activities could be implemented. This confidence seemed linked quite directly to a degree of independence from district mandates and some control over the budget that accompanied SBM. Parents, teachers, and administrators appeared to be quite willing to spend time identifying their needs and exploring ways to meet these because they had the sense that the implementation of these plans in an expeditious manner was under their control.

As we have noted, for teachers the fact that Jackson's initial foray into SBM coincided with their expressions of interest in Storyline training and with ready support of this activity was important. This almost seemed to startle teachers into the recognition that they could influence their own professional growth. Indeed, nine teachers mentioned that being able to ask for and receive good professional training was a factor in their ongoing support of LEARN.

By the time of our observations at Jackson, teachers seemed to almost take for granted that their needs would be acknowledged and that training would somehow be provided. For example, at one faculty meeting, teachers in grades two through five were quite vocal about their need to receive training in reading instruction, using principles similar to those in Reading Recovery. One even announced that she had already scheduled a meeting with a literacy expert to assist them in this effort. At the same meeting, another teacher emphasized that such training needed to extend to those who were working on developing literacy skills in Spanish with the goal of ultimately transitioning students into English. Several teachers commented on the need for additional training in the effective use of computers in their classrooms. At least five teachers spoke of their interest in more advanced Storyline training, and three individuals stated that they would like assistance in preparing students to take standardized tests in ways that would preserve their strong commitment to constructivist teaching and discovery learning. All of this discussion seemed to us to be based on the assumption that the faculty would, in fact, be able to receive all of the training they requested. Comments such as, "When we get advanced Storyline training, I'd like to participate" and "At our next pupil-free day, let's focus on test taking" were common.

Parents, on the other hand, did not appear to have a deeply embedded belief that the school would assist them. Nor did the ones we interviewed indicate a strong sense of agency and the belief that they could somehow create their own opportunities. They were, however, impressed with the open affirmations that parents were important partners in the educational process that came with the advent of LEARN and SBM. According to our informants, at first, parents responded to these statements and to the invitations to participate in governance and other school activities rather timidly. However, as the school responded to them, as administrators attended meetings at the Little Red Schoolhouse and worked with participants and others in the community to act on requests, the confidence and engagement of parents increased.

In addition to expediting Jackson's ability to provide professional learning opportunities and to increasing the engagement of teachers and parents in charting their own growth activities, the process of becoming an SBM school had another indirect impact on the development of capacity at this site. According to Leah Paul and several teachers, becoming a LEARN school was somewhat unsettling to many at this site because in the past, compliance with the principal and district had been the norm. Paul, as principal, was placed in a position where she was often as naive as teachers or parents about the processes of self-governance. She was thrust into the role of learner with them. As she embraced this role and worked with Mary Graves during the training provided by UCLA's School Management Program, according to two teachers, the custodian, and the office manager, she began to work more effectively with teachers in implementing SBM. The words of one veteran teacher were quite informative in this regard. She pointed out that "Mrs. [Paul's] personality is very strong in itself" and that she came from, I believe, an administrative, district-type situation into a school full of teachers who don't necessarily back down. She came in at a time when she had some teachers like myself who said, "You know what? This is my school and I've been here, and I'm gonna keep doing what I know works."

This teacher suggested that "the first couple of years, it was as difficult for her [Paul] to adjust as it was for all of us." She added, however, that Paul has grown as a leader and a colleague, and she attributed this both to her experiences at Jackson and to the training she has received as a LEARN school principal:

I've seen her back us on some pretty shaky deals. There have been some things that we've asked of her that she's like, "Well, . . ." but she's come through. I mean she has been a trooper. She's come through. Even though maybe personally I don't think she was sure if it would work, but she said, "You know what. I think you guys are professionals, and you know the school a little better than I do. I know the district, but you know the school; so you go with it, and I'll back you. I'll keep the district off of you. We are a LEARN school, and I'll support you; and if it works, hey, let's do it."

Paul's professional growth occurred in the context of SBM and of the training she received. It was not directly attributable to SBM as a governance structure, but it was an important side effect of Jackson's participation in reform efforts.

Although we did find a link between site autonomy and budgetary control and many dimensions of capacity-building activities, we did not detect a relationship between shared decision making and the quality of professional development. In the meetings we observed in which possible activities were discussed, teachers and administrators seemed to be coming to the table with well-developed ideas about the kinds of training they should pursue. These notions did not emerge from discussions at the site council meetings we observed. We learned from Paul that she and many of the teachers were continually "on the lookout" for good strategies and that several teachers were willing to join her to "engage in some good research about what would work here." And as we noted in Chapter 4, by her own admission, Paul would actively, albeit subtly, work to "sell" teachers on pedagogies she thought were especially promising.[4] We also overheard a number of conversations in which teachers discussed possible development activities. It seemed to us that consensus was often reached by teachers during these informal interactions.

□ Conclusions

At Jackson Elementary School, responding to the capacity-building imperative, effectively handling the demands of SBM, and successfully pursuing reform are linked in some interesting ways. In our view, SBM, although not a primary cause of the efficacious development activities or of transformation in learning and teaching, has played an important role in this area. The power of site autonomy at Jackson appears to be linked to two things. First, it has encouraged a sense of agency on the part of teachers and parents, and this, in turn, has fostered engagement in capacity-building activities. In the Los Angeles Unified School District, educators from many sites report that in the past they have felt that they had little control over their professional lives. They report being required to attend in-service workshops in order to comply with district, state, or federal mandates and note that these make little difference in the ways they teach. Furthermore, many teachers in this city complain that they are required to pay for any quality professional development and to pursue it on their own time, usually during summer vacations. In contrast, teachers at Jackson have the belief that their requests and self-identified needs will be addressed by the school and that additional training will be supported. A degree of autonomy and a measure of budgetary control seem to have made a difference in changing teachers' perceptions and experiences in this area. Under LEARN, principals and teachers can pursue professional development in ways that are more in line with the needs of their community.

A second benefit of SBM at Jackson in regard to professional development and school success is actually related to the first. Because the site has greater control over the ways it implements its site action plan, including its budget, the process of contracting and paying for professional development has been simplified. Only a few months elapsed between teachers' decision to pursue Scottish Storyline and their attendance at a training workshop. The same has been the case with other professional development efforts. This has certainly facilitated the quick adoption of new teaching strategies and, in a synergistic way, helped to keep enthusiasm and a spirit of innovation high.

It is important to note, however, that the high quality of capacity-building efforts at this site cannot be credited to SBM. The governance structure enabled decisions to be enacted, but it was not responsible for the goodness of those decisions. At Jackson, the choice of high-quality training activities seemed to be linked to the knowledge of instructional strategies possessed by Paul and a number of teachers and to their commitment to continuing learning in this area. There were, to be sure, numerous discussions in which ideas were shared and decisions negotiated. However, these did not occur in site council meetings. At this site, the settings for participation in this type of deliberation and decision making included collaborative planning times, faculty meetings, and numerous informal conversations held during the course of a typical day.

Our analysis of responses to the capacity-building imperative at Jackson suggests that SBM has been a central factor in facilitating effective development activities. However, we contend that the successful transformation that is underway here is also directly related to the high quality of decisions about the types of training that are needed. Furthermore, it is also linked to the enthusiastic participation of teachers, administrators, and parents in training activities. Knowledge and the commitment to continuous learning, especially on the part of the principal and several teachers, seem to be the factors most influential in ensuring that excellent and productive development activities are pursued. And the strong sense of community and commitment to student learning appear to be the forces that have done the most to shape high levels of participation and the willingness to implement ideas gained from training activities.

□ Notes

1. As we noted in Chapter 2, the commitment to give LEARN schools control over 80% of their budget preceded the actual release of information and funds. At the time Jackson decided to pursue Storyline training, Paul did not know exactly how much money was

available for them to apply to this training; however, her experience in the district and her general knowledge of resources for professional development gave her a sense of confidence that monies could be found to cover training in this area. Paul and at least two teachers offered the opinion that her previous work in the central office gave Jackson a great advantage, for Paul possessed what one teacher called "an insider's knowledge" of grants and other sources of support that could be tapped for professional development.

2. Storyline training is offered by a Canadian company. The cost for one participant at a 5-day session is $300. Substitutes in Los Angeles are paid approximately $100 per day.

3. Lynn Beck served as a faculty member for this program. Conceivably, information she received from Paul and Graves regarding the efficacy of this training might be influenced in some way by this fact. Two of the quotes reported here were given to Beck during interviews that occurred 2 years after Paul and Graves participated in the training. Others were provided to Cindy Kratzer, a research associate who had no connection with the School Management Program.

4. Paul and Graves were exposed to at least one of the teaching strategies, Scottish Storyline, during the Advanced Management Program offered by UCLA's School Management Program.

7

Success, the Four Imperatives, and SBM

We opened this book with a discussion of the logic of site-based management (SBM). Essentially, advocates of this form of governance assert that the devolution of authority and responsibility to local sites creates conditions that evoke high degrees of interest and engagement on the part of parents and teachers, who now feel empowered because they have a voice about resources allocation, personnel, and curriculum. This, in theory, leads to an increased sense of professionalism for educators and higher levels of participation for teachers, parents, and community members in the decision-making process. All of these factors, in turn, promote a healthy school organization and, ultimately, better workplace conditions for teachers, improved learning opportunities for students, and greater satisfaction for parents and community members.

As we contemplated the focus of the investigation reported here, we considered devising a study that would enable us to test this logic. We decided, however, to pursue a slightly different route and to undertake an effort to understand how SBM operated within a successful school. We felt that far too many investigations had focused on the policies aiming to create good schools. We wanted to focus on the school and to understand if and how a policy devolving power to the site worked with other factors to encourage a transformation of learning and teaching and improvements in parental involvement. We began by identifying a school—Jackson Elementary—that was both site managed and successful, according to a number of definitions of the term. We then participated in and observed this school community for an extended period of time, talking to a number of participants and analyzing documents that revealed some things about this institution's history to better understand forces that helped to shape its success and to see if and how SBM contributed to its transformation.

After analyzing data collected over months at this site, we have concluded that student learning, transformed teaching, and increasing parent involvement are due principally to responses at Jackson to four imperatives:

1. The imperative to promote learning—especially, but not exclusively—for students

2. The imperative for persons to assume leadership roles and to focus energies and resources of stakeholders in productive ways

3. The imperative to cultivate a sense of community within the school and to link the school with the larger community in mutually beneficial ways

4. The imperative to support efforts to build the capacity of administrators, teachers, and parents so that they are better able to support student learning

We have seen little to suggest that SBM is a primary force in shaping activities, values, and attitudes that have led to Jackson's success. We have, however, seen much to indicate that site autonomy has been meaningful in the presence of high levels of commitment to respond to the four imperatives. This governance structure has supported and facilitated the transformation of this school and its classes.

In this final chapter, we offer concluding thoughts about the interplay of forces shaping reform at Jackson Elementary School. We consider, first, the interplay of the four imperatives and suggest that the learning imperative provides an organizing center for the others. We then look at the power and limitations of SBM in supporting responses to the imperatives and school site success. Finally, we suggest some implications of our findings for school reform policies and practices.

☐ The Learning Imperative as the Organizing Center

Comprehensive educational reform is a complicated endeavor—especially if it involves shifting control and responsibility away from a centralized authority to local sites. Persons interested in promoting positive change within local schools must contend with the inherent "intractability" (Sarason, 1990, p. 110) of educational institutions. They must also reckon with the reality that, in reform efforts involving site autonomy and shared decision making, the complex tasks of administering and teaching are in some ways made even more complicated by dual realities that management tasks, once handled by a centralized agency, are relegated to the site and that a host of persons, many of whom have had little experience in educational decision making, must be involved in governance. Furthermore, if an autonomous site takes seriously the challenge of reform, administrators, teachers, and parents must find ways to go beyond maintenance of the status quo to a state characterized by improved learning outcomes and organizational transformation.

Some research suggests that the combination of multiple tasks and multiple decision makers can have a disorganizing effect within schools. Governance councils find themselves dealing with a host of issues, many of which have little relationship to the core work of schools (e.g., Collins & Hanson, 1991; David, 1993; Hill & Bonan, 1991; Sackney & Dibski, 1992). Furthermore, "teachers report that involvement in committee work distracts teachers' energy away from teaching, correction, and classroom practice" (Chapman, 1990, p. 237). Not only does "the shifting of management responsibilities to the school level [create] in some way a distraction from the central process of schooling" (Caldwell, 1990, p. 20), it also creates major time pressures for educators. And large numbers of parents, in many instances, have not jumped at opportunities to be involved in reform-oriented governance (Bradley, 1993; David, 1993; Hess, 1992). The reasons for this, in all likelihood, vary, but it seems likely that the time demands are also a problem for parents. In some cases, they feel that they lack the requisite knowledge for making educational decisions, and in others, parents believe that deliberations about schooling are properly and appropriately made by educational professionals (Weiss, Cambone, & Wyeth, 1992).

At Jackson Elementary School, we saw little that suggested that the pulls and pressures of self-management and reform were draining the energy of educators or distracting them from the core work of schools. This seemed to be due in part to the primacy of the learning imperative at this site. The belief that learning was important, exciting, and accessible was so pervasive that it almost seemed to be woven into the culture of Jackson. This idea and projects emanating from it provided a strong center for much of the activity at this site, and in so doing, it helped to bring a sense of coherence to the site.

It appeared to us that the commitment to good teaching and powerful learning served as a kind of lens to focus and concentrate the attention and energies of decision makers at this site. As we point out above, governing bodies at SBM schools have a tendency to become distracted by a plethora of needs and issues. At Jackson, the topics discussed at the faculty and site council meetings we attended were, for the most part, related directly to teaching and learning.

Not only did the learning imperative appear to shape the agendas of governance meetings, but it also gave meaning and an overarching purpose to many of the other activities at this site. Leadership efforts, as we noted in Chapter 4, were often aimed at improving the educational climate at this site. Parental outreach efforts centered around the provision of learning opportunities, and many of these were designed to enable parents to join educators in ensuring that their children did well in school. And the vast majority of capacity-building efforts, formal and informal, in-house and off-site, were aimed at providing teachers with the knowledge and skills to enable them to work well with every child at Jackson. In a certain sense, the learning imperative at this site seemed to us to function as the imperatives' imperative. It focused resources, governance, outreach efforts, professional development, and more directly on making "an impact on what [and how] students learn in school" (Elmore, 1993, p. 39).

□ The Role of SBM

Even though we saw little evidence of SBM's direct effect on outcomes at Jackson Elementary School, we did discover several ways in which this aspect of this governance structure contributed to school success. The relative autonomy from the Los Angeles Unified School District, in our view, was a more powerful factor in creating conditions that fostered transformation than was participatory decision making, but the latter dimension of SBM also had some effect on events at Jackson.

The autonomy from the district that is afforded to LEARN schools was a great energizer at Jackson. Over and over in conversations, we heard statements such as "Hey, we can do this. We're a LEARN school" and "After all, we can try it. We're a LEARN school." The excitement that accompanied this perception of freedom from the central office needs to be understood within the context of Los Angeles, where for some years the district has been viewed by most teachers and by many administrators as excessively bureaucratic and controlling. This, according to analysts of schooling in this city (Bates, 1995; Kindy, 1995), has undermined teachers' morale and squelched risk taking for many educators. For many faculty members, the fact that they and their colleagues could do much to establish goals and design strategies to meet them with the support of the school board and school district administrators was a heady experience.

In addition to creating a sense of agency on the part of teachers at Jackson, autonomy from the district had another important benefit for this site. Under the centralized management structure that preceded LEARN, there was a significant time lag between the making of any decision and the actual implementation of it. Contracts, purchase orders, requests, and reports frequently generated multiple forms that had to be sent through the system for approval before any action could be taken at the site. Often the situation generating the decision in the first place changed by the time of its implementation. As an SBM school, Jackson had the authority to act quickly on its own plans. For example, when teachers decided that they wanted Storyline training, Paul and the other administrators immediately set out to arrange this, knowing that they could somehow find resources to pay for it. Thus, a set of purchases authorized by the site council in November had been made by early January. Similarly, plans for Tuesday morning parent meetings that were made in October were immediately put into place; within days of parents' requesting a type of class at the Little Red Schoolhouse, administrators and the parent liaison had located an instructor and scheduled the class.

Formal structures established for shared decision making at Jackson seemed to us to have little impact on the participation of teachers in deliberations about instruction, resources, and schedules. This is probably due to two things—the culture of this site and the fact that teachers had a choice about participating in most activities even when decisions were made. We have written at length about the conversations about educational issues that occurred in a variety of different settings—the collaborative planning meetings, hallway conversations, the lunchroom, faculty meetings, and social settings. Frequently, there emerged from these a sense of consensus about a pedagogy or curriculum. At other times, issues were delineated as a result of teachers' conversations so that representatives to the site council could present a limited and focused set of issues or questions for discussion. Even when a decision was reached by the council or some other group, teachers at Jackson typically could decide whether or not they would participate in its implementation. When, for example, the council endorsed a hands-on mathematics curriculum, a few teachers opted not to embrace this. We can imagine that leaving choices about implementation up to teachers could present problems, but thus far Jackson seems to have escaped them. Most individuals, in fact, seem to agree, in general, about teaching strategies and classroom materials. The few who differ from the others on some issue appear to have a good relationship with their colleagues and a strong commitment to the children, and they work with both to see that students do not pay the price for differences among teachers.

In contrast to teachers, at least a few parents indicated that their relationship with the school had changed as a result of having structures in which they were invited and expected to participate in governance. We rarely saw parents speaking at these meetings, but we learned in interviews with some who had participated that their confidence and sense of power was increasing. Furthermore, they told us of sharing their experiences with other parents and encouraging them to realize that they could do something about their child's education if they would become involved at the site.

Ultimately, we concluded that at this site, concerted attention to the four imperatives with a special focus on learning was the major contributor to the success of Jackson Elementary School. We found SBM to be important in creating conditions that facilitated the ability of persons at this site to act on their commitments to learning, leadership, community, and capacity building.

□ Implications

Our time at Jackson has prompted us to join the crowing chorus of individuals (e.g., Elmore, 1993, 1995; Tyack, 1993) who question the emphasis of school reformers on policy and structure. We found little evidence to suggest that anything inherent in SBM caused Leah Paul, other administrators, and the teachers at Jackson to be strongly committed to changing practice to promote higher levels of learning for all students. Neither did we see SBM contributing to the ability of individuals at this site to make good decisions about instructional strategies, curricula, and professional development. Yet the commitment to effective, developmentally sound instruction and the knowledge and will to discover and implement pedagogies that support this commitment and to encourage high levels of learning for all children were the factors that, in our view, were most responsible for this site's transformation.

These conclusions prompt us to suggest that advocates of reform might do well to follow the recommendations of Michael Fullan (1991) to consider ways to influence the deeply embedded commitments and professional knowledge of educators. We suspect that policies will not serve as an effective vehicle for influencing such commitments. Indeed, our investigation into Jackson's successful transformation, buttressed by research on school change (e.g., Elmore, Peterson, & McCarthy, 1996; Fullan, 1991; Sarason, 1991) suggests that values, beliefs, and perceptions cannot be mandated but that they can be cultivated, encouraged, and nurtured. We would argue that policies should focus on creating the conditions that allow individuals concerned about providing children and adults with powerful learning opportunities to act on their commitments. We have already hinted at what some of those conditions might be. We suspect they would include support for risk taking; freedom from excessive bureaucratic constraints; and time, money, and administrative support for substantive professional development.

The importance of professional development in reform cannot, in our view, be underestimated. While we were at Jackson, we were impressed again and again with the fact that people at this site were not merely making decisions. They were making *instructionally sound* decisions. The instructional strategies chosen by educators were, in our view, theoretically sound; and more important, they were working. Teachers were excited, parents were satisfied, and students were engaged in learning and demonstrating growth in problem solving and communication skills. We would argue that high-quality pre- and inservice professional development—chosen, if possible, by teachers committed to their students and their craft—is critical if SBM or any other reform effort is to work.

There are many vehicles for the development of knowledge and skills for teachers, administrators, and parents. We would assert, however, that training activities that are theoretically grounded— that go beyond mere technique and prompt educators to think analytically about practice and to search continually for a clearer understanding of problems and a richer set of solutions—are needed. Others, we fear, will fail to equip teachers and administrators to respond to the quickly changing environments in which they work and their students live.

We recognize the impossibility of generalizing from a single case study. However, we can state that our investigation at Jackson Elementary School has not dissuaded us from a conclusion we expressed in an earlier manuscript (Murphy & Beck, 1995): SBM "is a fairly weak intervention in our arsenal of school reform measures" (p. 178). We have, however, come to appreciate the usefulness of SBM for a school with certain characteristics. These center on a commitment to promoting high levels of learning for all students. They also include the presence of supportive, informed, and focused leaders; the persistent cultivation of a sense of community within the school and between the school, parents, and others in the larger environment; and resources and the willingness to invest them to support substantial and appropriate development for all stakeholders. If these characteristics exist in schools, we would argue that they possess a solid foundation for successful transformation. At such schools, SBM is likely to be profitable. If these commitments are not in place, then we would call on policymakers at state and local levels to consider seriously their reasons for supporting site autonomy. Our realization that SBM enables individual schools to act more quickly and decisively is exciting if persons at that site are making sound decisions. However, it is frightening if teachers, parents, and administrators decide on teaching and curricular strategies and approaches to student discipline, personnel hiring and evaluation systems, admissions policies, and approaches to parental and community involvement that undermine good learning and healthy development and are insensitive, disrespectful to persons or groups, or fundamentally unjust.

It seems to us that a good starting point for policymakers on all levels of the system would be a consideration of their goals for a decentralized school system. If they are interested merely in altering power structures in educational systems, SBM is a viable structure to pursue. By its nature, it shifts power from certain levels of the system to others. If reformers are concerned about creating schools that function more democratically, then SBM—if it includes genuine participatory decision making—again, may be a promising organizational approach. If, however, the goal of devolving power to a local site is to improve student learning, then we would contend that reformers should be reasonably certain that the will to make changes; the knowledge about promising directions; and leadership, community support, and resources for extensive and intensive stakeholder development are present. If such conditions are not evident, persons concerned with reform might find focusing on creating conditions that foster the spirit and ability of the imperatives of promoting learning, developing leadership, cultivating community, and building capacity to be a more productive use of their efforts.

References

Alexander, G. C. (1992, April). *The transformation of an urban principal: Uncertain times, uncertain roles.* Paper presented at the annual meeting of the American Educational Research Association, San Francisco, CA.

American Association for the Advancement of the Teaching of Science. (1984). *A report on the crisis in mathematics and science education: What can be done now?* New York: J. C. Crimmins.

Anderson, G. L., & Dixon, A. (1993). Paradigm shifts and site-based management in the United States: Toward a paradigm of social empowerment. In J. Smyth (Ed.), *A socially critical view of the self-managing school* (pp. 49-61). London: Taylor & Francis.

Bachus, G. S. (1991, October). *The shifting format of administration in small schools: Participatory school decision making.* Paper presented at the annual conference of the National Rural Education Association, Jackson, MS.

Barth, R. S. (1990). *Improving schools from within: Teachers, parents, and principals can make the difference.* San Francisco: Jossey-Bass.

Beck, L. G., & Murphy, J. (1993). *Understanding the principalship: Metaphorical themes, 1920s-1990s.* New York: Teachers College Press.

Bestor, A. (1953). *Educational wastelands: The retreat from learning in our public schools.* Urbana: University of Illinois Press.

Bickman, L. (1987). The functions of program theory. In L. Bickman (Ed.), *Using program theory in evaluation* (pp. 5-18). San Francisco: Jossey-Bass.

Bimber, B. (1993). *School decentralization: Lessons from the study of bureaucracy.* Santa Monica, CA: RAND.

Boyd, W. L., & O'Shea, D. W. (1975). Theoretical perspectives on school district restructuring. *Education and Urban Society, 7*(4), 464-479.

Boyer, E. (1983). *High school.* New York: Harper & Row.

Bradley, A. (1993). Shortcomings of decentralized decisionmaking in NYC detailed. *Education Week, 13*(6), 14.

Brown, D. J. (1990). *Decentralization and school-based management.* London: Falmer.

Brown, D. J. (1991). *Decentralization: The administrator's guidebook to school district change.* Newbury Park, CA: Corwin.

Brown, T., & Lindle, J. C. (1995). *Undercurrents in consensus: A case study.* Lexington: University of Kentucky/University of Louisville Joint Center on Educational Policy.

Bryk, A. S. (1993). *A view from the elementary schools: The state of reform in Chicago.* Chicago: Chicago Consortium on School Research.

Bryk, A. S., & Driscoll, M. E. (1988). *The school as community: Theoretical foundations, contextual influences, and consequences for students and teachers* (Report WP 88-11-05). Chicago: University of Chicago Benton Center for Research in Curriculum and Instruction.

Bryk, A. S., Lee, V. E., & Holland, P. B. (1993). *Catholic schools and the common good.* Cambridge, MA: Harvard University Press.

Burke, C. (1992). Devolution of responsibility to Queensland schools: Clarifying the rhetoric critiquing the reality. *Journal of Educational Administration, 30*(4), 33-52.

Business-Higher Education Forum. (1983). *America's competitive challenge.* Washington, DC: Author.

Caldwell, B. (1990). School-based decision-making and management: International developments. In J. Chapman (Ed.), *School-based decision-making and management* (pp. 3-26). London: Falmer.

Carnegie Forum on Education and the Economy. (1986). *A nation prepared.* Washington DC: Author.

Carnoy, M., & MacDonnell, J. (1990). School district restructuring in Santa Fe, New Mexico. *Educational Policy, 4*(1), 49-64.

Center for the Future of Children. (1992). *The future of children: School linked services*. Los Altos, CA: Author.

Chapman, J. (1990). School-based decision-making and management: Implications for school personnel. In J. Chapman (Ed.), *School-based decision-making and management* (pp. 221-244). London: Falmer.

Chapman, J., & Boyd, W. L. (1986). Decentralization, devolution, and the school principal: Australian lessons on statewide educational reform. *Educational Administration Quarterly, 22*(4), 28-58.

Chasin, G., & Levin, H. (1995). Thomas Edison Accelerated Elementary School. In J. Oakes & K. H. Quartz (Eds.), *Creating new educational communities: Ninety-fourth yearbook of the National Society for the Study of Education* (pp. 130-146). Chicago: University of Chicago Press.

Chubb, J. E., & Moe, T. M. (1990). *Politics, markets, and America's schools*. Washington, DC: Brookings Institute.

Clark, D. L., & Meloy, J. M. (1989). Renouncing bureaucracy: A democratic structure for leadership in schools. In T. J. Sergiovanni & J. A. Moore (Eds.), *Schooling for tomorrow: Directing reform to issues that count* (pp. 272-294). Boston: Allyn & Bacon.

Clune, W. H., & White, P. A. (1988). *School-based management: Institutional variation, implementation, and issues for further research*. New Brunswick, NJ: Rutgers University, Eagleton Institute of Politics, Center for Policy Research in Education.

Collins, O. T. (1994). *Emerging central office roles in a decentralizing school district*. Unpublished doctoral dissertation, Vanderbilt University, Nashville, TN.

Collins, R. A., & Hanson, J. K. (1991). *School-based management/shared decision-making project 1987-88 through 1989-90: Summative evaluation report*. Miami, FL: Dade County Public Schools, Office of Educational Accountability.

Comer, J. (1980). *School power*. New York: Free Press.

Comer, J. (1986). Parent participation in the schools. *Phi Delta Kappan, 67*, 442-446.

Comer, J. (1988). Child development and education. *Journal of Negro Education, 58*, 125-139.

Committee for Economic Development. (1987). *Children in need: Investment strategies for the educationally disadvantaged*. New York: Author.

Committee for Economic Development. (1991). *Unfinished agenda.* New York: Author.

Conley, D. T. (1991). Lessons from laboratories in school restructuring and site-based decision making. *Oregon School Study Council Bulletin, 34*(7), 1-61.

Conway, J. A. (1984). The myth, mystery, and mastery of participative decision making in education. *Educational Administration Quarterly, 20*(3), 11-40.

Conway, J., & Calzi, F. (1995). The dark side of shared decision making. *Educational Leadership, 53*(4), 45-49.

Corbett, D., & Wilson, B. (1995). Make a difference with, not for students: A plea to researchers and reformers. *Educational Researcher, 24*(3), 12-17.

Crosby, S. (1991). *Teachers' opinions of school-based management.* ERIC Document Reproduction Service No. ED 343 241 EA 023785.

Daresh, J. C. (1992). Impressions of school-based management: The Cincinnati story. In J. J. Lane & E. G. Epps (Eds.), *Restructuring the schools: Problems and prospects* (pp. 109-121). Berkeley, CA: McCutchan.

Darling-Hammond, L. (1988). Policy and professionalism. In A. Lieberman (Ed.), *Building a professional culture in schools* (pp. 55-77). New York: Teachers College Press.

David, J. L. (1989). Synthesis of research on school-based management. *Educational Leadership, 46*(8), 45-53.

David, J. L. (1993, August). *School-based decision making: Progress and promise.* Paper presented to the Prichard Committee (KY) for Academic Excellence.

David, J. L. (1995). The who, what, and why of site-based management. *Educational Leadership, 53*(4), 4-9.

Dellar, G. B. (1992, April). *Connections between macro and micro implementation of educational policy: A study of school restructuring in Western Australia.* Paper presented at the annual meeting of the American Educational Research Association, San Francisco, CA.

Des Carpentrie, K. M. (1995). *The role of parents in a school-based management council.* Unpublished doctoral dissertation, Vanderbilt University, Nashville, TN.

Dewey, J. (1900). *The school and society.* Chicago: University of Chicago Press.

Dewey, J. (1966). *Democracy and education.* New York: Macmillan.

Duke, D. L., Showers, B., & Imber, M. (1980). Teachers and shared decision-making: The costs and benefits of involvement. *Educational Administration Quarterly, 16*(1), 93-106.

Duttweiler, P. C., & Mutchler, S. E. (1990). *Organizing the educational system for excellence: Harnessing the energy of people.* Austin, TX: Southwest Educational Development Laboratory.

Eastin, D. (1995, August). *LEARN summit address.* Los Angeles, CA.

Easton, J. (1991). *Decision making and school improvement.* Chicago: Chicago Panel on Public School Policy and Finance.

Edmonds, R. (1979). Effective schools for the urban poor. *Educational Leadership, 37*(1), 15-24.

Elmore, K., Peterson, P., & McCarthy, S. (1996). *Restructuring the classroom: Teaching, learning, and school organization.* San Francisco: Jossey-Bass.

Elmore, R. F. (1993). School decentralization: Who gains? Who loses? In J. Hannaway & M. Carnoy (Eds.), *Decentralization and school improvement* (pp. 33-54). San Francisco: Jossey-Bass.

Elmore, R. F. (1995). Structural reform in educational practice. *Educational Researcher, 24*(9), 23-26.

Etheridge, C. P., Hall, M. L., & Brown, N. (1990, January). *Leadership, control, communication, and comprehension: Key factors in successful implementation of SBDM.* Paper presented at the annual meeting of the Mid-South Educational Research Association, New Orleans, LA.

Flax, E. (1989a). South Carolina adopts regulatory relief for high scoring schools. *Education Week, 9*(12), 1, 16.

Flax, E. (1989b). South Carolina considering "flexibility" for top scoring schools. *Education Week, 10*(39), 13.

Fullan, M. (1991). *The new meaning of educational change.* New York: Teachers College Press.

Fullan, M. (1993). Coordinating school and district development. In J. Murphy & P. Hallinger (Eds.), *Restructuring schooling: Learning from ongoing efforts* (pp. 143-164). Newbury Park, CA: Corwin.

Fusarelli, L. C., & Scribner, J. D. (1993, October). *Site-based management and critical democratic pluralism: An analysis of promises, problems, and possibilities.* Paper presented at the University Council for Educational Administration, Houston, TX.

Gailbrath, J. R. (1977). *Organizational design.* Reading, MA: Addison-Wesley.

Gardner, H. (1991). *The unschooled mind: How children think and how schools should teach.* New York: Basic Books.

Garms, W., Guthrie, J., & Pierce, L. (1978). *School finance: The economics and politics of education.* Englewood Cliffs, NJ: Prentice Hall.

Geraci, B. (1995). Local decision making: A report from the trenches. *Educational Leadership, 53*(4), 50-53.

Gips, C. J., & Wilkes, M. (1993, April). *Teacher concerns as they consider an organization change to site-based decision making.* Paper presented at the annual meeting of the American Educational Research Association, Atlanta, GA.

Goldman, P., Dunlap, D. M., & Conley, D. T. (1991, April). *Administrative facilitation and site-based school reform projects.* Paper presented at the annual meeting of the American Educational Research Association, Chicago.

Graham, P. (1984). Schools: Cacophony about practice, silence about purpose. *Dadaelus, 113*(4), 29-57.

Guskey, T. R., & Peterson, K. D. (1995). The road to classroom change. *Educational Leadership, 53*(4), 10-15.

Guthrie, J. W. (1986). School-based management: The next needed education reform. *Phi Delta Kappan, 68*(4), 305-309.

Guttierez, K., & Meyer, B. (1995). Creating communities of effective practice: Building literacy for language minority students. In J. Oakes & K. H. Quartz (Eds.), *Creating new educational communities: Ninety-fourth Yearbook of the National Society for the Study of Education* (pp. 32-51). Chicago: University of Chicago Press.

Hallinger, P., Murphy, J., & Hausman, C. (1992). Restructuring schools: Principals' perceptions of fundamental educational reform. *Educational Administration Quarterly, 28*(3), 330-339.

Halpern, R. (1990). *Supportive services for families in poverty: Historical perspectives, dilemmas of reform.* Chicago: Erikson Institute.

Hannaway, J. (1992). *Decentralization in education: Technical demands as a critical ingredient.* ERIC Document Reproduction Service No. ED 345 362.

Hannaway, J. (1993). Decentralization in two school districts: Challenging the standard paradigm. In J. Hannaway & M. Carnoy (Eds.), *Decentralization and school improvement: Can we fulfill the promise?* (pp. 135-162). San Francisco: Jossey-Bass.

Hanson, E. M. (1991). *School-based management and educational reform: Cases in the USA and Spain.* ERIC Document Reproduction Service No. ED 345 362.

Hanson, M. (1991, April). *Alteration of influence relations in school-based management.* Paper presented at the annual meeting of the American Educational Research Association, Chicago.

Harp, L. (1993). Widely mixed test results leave some in Kentucky puzzled. *Education Week, 13*(6), 15.

Heckman, P. E., Confer, C., & Peacock, J. (1995). Democracy in a multicultural school and community. In J. Oakes & K. H. Quartz (Eds.), *Creating new educational communities: Ninety-fourth yearbook of the National Society for the Study of Education* (pp. 187-202). Chicago: University of Chicago Press.

Herriman, M. (1995). Democratic values, individual rights, and personal freedom in education. In J. Chapman, I. Froumin, & D. Aspin (Eds.), *Creating and managing the democratic school* (pp. 176-193). London: Falmer.

Hess, G. A. (1992). *School restructuring, Chicago style: A midway report.* Chicago: Chicago Panel on Public School Policy.

Hill, P. T., & Bonan, J. (1991). *Decentralization and accountability in public education.* Santa Monica, CA: RAND.

Hirsch, E. D. (1987). *Cultural literacy.* Boston: Houghton Mifflin.

Hodgkinson, H. (1989). *The same client: The demographics of education and service delivery systems.* Washington, DC: Institute for Educational Leadership, Inc., Center for Demographic Policy.

Honig, B. (1985). *Last chance for our children.* Reading, MA: Addison-Wesley.

Hume, W. S. (1996, Jan. 8). Slavkin on state education code. *Los Angeles Times*, p. M-4.

Jackson, D. (1996). *Los Angeles principals and LEARN: An analysis of beliefs.* Unpublished doctoral dissertation, University of California, Los Angeles.

Jehl, J., & Kirst, M. (1992). Getting ready to provide school-linked services: What schools must do. In R. E. Behrman (Ed.), *The future of children: School-linked services* (pp. 95-106). Los Altos, CA: Center for the Future of Children.

Jenni, R. W. (1990, April). *Application of school based management process development general model.* Paper presented at the annual meeting of the American Educational Research Association, Boston.

Jenni, R. W., & Mauriel, J. J. (1990, April). *An examination of factors affecting stakeholders' assessment of school decentralization.* Paper presented at the annual meeting of the American Educational Research Association, Boston.

Jewell, K. E., & Rosen, J. L. (1993, April). *School-based management/shared decision-making: A study of school reform in New York City.* Paper presented at the annual meeting of the American Educational Research Association, Atlanta, GA.

Kearnes, D., & Doyle, D. P. (1988). *Winning the brain race: A bold plan to make our schools competitive.* San Francisco: ICS Press.

Kindy, K. (1995, June 11). [Jackson] school LEARNS meaning of hope for future. *The Daily News,* pp. 1, 3, 14-15.

Krechevsky, M., Hoerr, T., & Gardner, H. (1995). Complementary energies: Implementing MI theory from the laboratory and from the field. In J. Oakes & K. H. Quartz (Eds.), *Creating new educational communities: Ninety-fourth yearbook of the National Society for the Study of Education* (pp. 166-186). Chicago: University of Chicago Press.

La Noue, G. R., & Smith, B. L. R. (1973). *The politics of school decentralization.* Lexington, MA: Lexington Press.

Lawrence, S. (1996). *Power, roles and relationships: Secondary principals' response to reform.* Unpublished doctoral dissertation, University of California, Los Angeles.

Lawton, S. B. (1991, April). *Why restructure?* Paper presented at the annual meeting of the American Educational Research Association, Chicago.

LEARN. (1994), *Revised site action plan, [Jackson] Elementary School: 1994-1997.* Unpublished document.

Levin, H. (1987). Accelerated schools for disadvantaged students. *Educational Leadership, 44*(6), 19-21.

Levin, H. (1991). Accelerated visions. *Accelerated Schools, 1*(3), 2.

Levine, D. U., & Eubanks, E. E. (1992). Site-based management: Engine of reform or pipedream? Problems, prospects, pitfalls, and prerequisites for success. In J. J. Lane & E. G. Epps (Eds.), *Restructuring the schools: Problems and prospects* (pp. 61-82). Berkeley, CA: McCutchan.

Lewis, D. A. (1993). Deinstitutionalization and school decentralization: Making the same mistake twice. In J. Hannaway & M. Carnoy (Eds.), *Decentralization and school improvement* (pp. 84-101). San Francisco: Jossey-Bass.

Lieberman, A., Falk, B., & Alexander, L. (1995). A culture in the making: Leadership in learner-centered schools. In J. Oakes & K. H. Quartz (Eds.), *Creating new educational communities: Ninety-fourth yearbook of the National Society for the Study of Education* (pp. 108-129). Chicago: University of Chicago Press.

Lightfoot, S. L. (1984). *The good high school.* New York: Basic Books.

Lindelow, J. (1981). School-based management. In S. C. Smith, J. A. Massarella, & P. K. Piele (Eds.), *School leadership: Handbook for survival* (pp. 94-129). Eugene: University of Oregon, ERIC Clearinghouse on Educational Management.

Lindle, J. C. (1992). *The implementation of the Kentucky Education Reform Act: A descriptive study of the parent involvement provisions.* Unpublished report, University of Kentucky at Lexington.

Lindle, J. C., Gale, B. S., & Currywhite, B. S. (1994). *School-based decision making: 1994 survey.* Frankfort: Kentucky Department of Education and the University of Kentucky/University of Louisville Joint Center for the Study of Educational Policy.

Lindquist, K. M., & Mauriel, J. J. (1989). School-based management: Doomed to failure? *Education and Urban Society, 21*(4), 403-416.

Lohman, D. F. (1993). Teaching and testing to develop fluid abilities. *Educational Researcher, 22*(7), 12-23.

Louis, K. S., & Murphy, J. (1994). The evolving role of the principal: Some concluding thoughts. In Murphy, J., & Louis, K. S. (Eds.), *Reshaping the principalship: Insights from transformational reform efforts* (pp. 265-281). Thousand Oaks, CA: Corwin.

Malen, B., & Ogawa, R. T. (1988). Professional-patron influence on site-based governance councils: A confounding case study. *Educational Evaluation and Policy Analysis, 10*(4), 251-270.

Malen, B., Ogawa, R. T., & Kranz, J. (1989, May). *What do we know about school based management: A case study of the literature—A call for research.* Paper presented at the Conference on Choice and Control in American Education, University of Wisconsin, Madison.

March, J. G., & Olson, J. P. (1983). What administrative reorganization tells us about governing. *American Political Science Review, 77*(2), 281-296.

Marsh, D. (1992). *Change in schools.* ERIC Document Reproduction Service No. ED 353 673.

Marshall, K. (1995, August). *Assessing learning outcomes.* Presentation at Advanced Management Program Summer Institute for LEARN Phase II Schools, Palm Springs, CA.

Mathland. (n.d.). *Journeys through mathematics.* Worth, IL: Creative Publications.

McCarthy, J., & Still, S. (1993). Hollibrook accelerated elementary school. In J. Murphy & P. Hallinger (Eds.), *Restructuring schooling: Learning from ongoing efforts* (pp. 63-83). Newbury Park, CA: Corwin.

McDonough, J. (1993, July). *Dedicated behavior for educators.* Paper presented at the Advanced Management Program Summer Institute, Pomona, CA.

McKinsey & Co. (1994). *LEARN progress assessment.* Report prepared for the LEARN Working Group, Los Angeles.

Metz, M. H. (1986). *Different by design: The context and character of three magnet schools.* New York: Routledge & Kegan Paul.

Miles, M. B. (1969). *Planned change and organizational health.* In F. D. Carter & T. J. Sergiovanni (Eds.), *Organization and human behavior: Focus on schools* (pp. 375-399). New York: McGraw-Hill.

Mirel, J. (1990). What history can teach us about school decentralization. *Network News and Views, 9*(8), 40-47.

Mohrman, S. A. (1994). High-involvement management in the private sector. In S. A. Mohrman, P. Wohlstetter, & Associates (Eds.), *School-based management: Organizing for high performance* (pp. 25-52). San Francisco: Jossey-Bass.

Mojkowski, C., & Fleming, D. (1988). *School-site management: Concepts and approaches.* Andover, MA: Regional Laboratory for the Educational Improvement of the Northeast and Islands.

Murphy, J. (1990). The educational reform movement of the 1980s: A comprehensive analysis. In J. Murphy (Ed.), *The reform of American public education in 1980s: Perspectives and cases* (pp. 3-57). Berkeley: McCutchan.

Murphy, J. (1991). *Restructuring schools: Capturing and assessing the phenomenon.* New York: Teachers College Press.

Murphy, J. (1992). School effectiveness and school restructuring: Contributions to educational improvement. *School Effectiveness and School Improvement, 3*(2), 90-109.

Murphy, J. (1994). Transformational change and the evolving role of the principalship: Early empirical evidence. In J. Murphy & K. S. Louis (Eds.), *Reshaping the principalship: Insights from trans-*

formational reform efforts (pp. 20-53). Thousand Oaks, CA: Corwin.

Murphy, J. (1995). Restructuring in Kentucky: The changing role of the superintendent and district office. In K. A. Leithwood (Ed.), *Effective school district leadership: Transforming politics into education.* Albany: State University of New York Press.

Murphy, J. (1996). *Privatization policy: Framing the school reform debate.* Thousand Oaks, CA: Corwin.

Murphy, J., & Beck, L. G. (1995). *School-based management as school reform: Taking stock.* Thousand Oaks, CA: Corwin.

Murphy, J., & Hallinger, P. (1993). Restructuring schooling: Learning from ongoing efforts. In J. Murphy & P. Hallinger (Eds.), *Restructuring schooling: Learning from ongoing efforts* (pp. 251-271). Newbury Park, CA: Corwin.

Murphy, J., Hallinger, P., & Mesa, R. P. (1985). School effectiveness: Checking progress and assumptions and developing a role for state and federal government. *Teachers College Record, 86*(4), 615-641.

Murphy, J., Weil, M., Hallinger, P., & Mitman, A. (1982). Academic press: Translating high expectations into school policies and classroom practices. *Educational Leadership, 40*(3), 22-26.

Murphy, J. T. (1989). The paradox of decentralizing schools: Lessons from business, government, and the Catholic Church. *Phi Delta Kappan, 70,* 808-812.

Mutchler, S. E., & Duttweiller, P. C. (1990, April). *Implementing shared decision making in school based management: Barriers to changing traditional behavior.* Paper presented at the annual meeting of the American Educational Research Association, Boston.

National Commission on Excellence in Education. (1983). *A nation at risk: The imperative of educational reform.* Washington, DC: Author.

National Science Board. (1983). *Educating Americans for the 21st century.* Washington DC: Author.

Neill, G. (1981, December 21). President Reagan values education, Meese proclaims. *Education Week,* p. 1.

Newmann, F. (1993). Beyond common sense in educational restructuring: The issues of content and linkage. *Educational Researcher, 22*(2), 4-13.

Notes from the field. (1991). *Special feature: School-based decision-making* (Vol. 1, No. 2). Charleston, SC: Appalachia Educational Laboratory.

Olson, L. (1991a). Dallas schools seek to streamline bureaucracy. *Education Week, 10*(16), 9.

Olson, L. (1991b). Effort to cut back D.C.'s bureaucracy proves net-tlesome. *Education Week, 11*(12), 1, 18-19.

Olson, L. (1992). A matter of choice: Minnesota puts "charter schools" ideas to test. *Education Week, 12*(12), 1, 10-11.

Ornstein, A. C. (1983). Administrative decentralization and community policy: Review and outlook. *Urban Review, 15*(1), 3-10.

Ovando, M. N. (1993). *Effects of site-based management on the instructional program.* Paper presented at the annual meeting of the University Council for Educational Administration, Houston, TX.

Pacific Region Educational Laboratory. (1992). *Evaluation of implementation of school/community management: Final report.* Honolulu, HI: Author.

Perkins, D. (1992). Inside understanding. In D. Perkins (Ed.), *Teaching for understanding in an age of technology.*

Perkins, D. (1995). *Outsmarting IQ: The emerging science of learnable intelligence.* New York: Free Press.

Perkins, D., & Blythe, T. (1994). Putting understanding up front. *Educational Leadership, 51*(5), 4-7.

Powell, A. G., Farrar, E., & Cohen, D. K. (1985). *The shopping mall high school: Winners and losers in the educational marketplace.* Boston: Houghton Mifflin.

Prickett, R. L., Flangian, J. L., Richardson, M. D., & Petrie, G. F. (1990, October). *Who knows what? Site-based management.* Paper presented at the annual meeting of the University Council for Educational Administration, Baltimore, MD.

Purkey, S. C., & Smith, M. S. (1983). Effective schools: A review. *Elementary Schools Journal, 83*, 427-452.

Rice, E. M., & Schneider, G. T. (1992, April). *A decade of teacher empowerment: An empirical analysis of teacher involvement in decision making.* Paper presented at the annual meeting of the American Educational Research Association, San Francisco, CA.

Robertson, P., & Briggs, K. (1995, April). *The impact of school-based management on educators' role attitudes and behaviors.* Paper presented at the annual meeting of the American Educational Research Association, San Francisco, CA.

Rogers, D. (1981). *School decentralization in New York City.* ERIC Document Reproduction Service No. ED 219 466.

Rosenholtz, S. J. (1991). *Teachers' workplace: The social organization of schools.* New York: Teachers College Press.

Rungeling, B., & Glover, R. W. (1991). Educational restructuring—The process for change? *Urban Education, 25*(4), 415-427.

Rutherford, B. (1991, April). *School-based management and school improvement: How it happened in three school districts.* Paper presented at the annual meeting of the American Educational Research Association, Chicago.

Rutter, M., Maughan, B., Mortimore, P., & Ouston, J. (1979). *Fifteen thousand hours: Secondary schools and their effects on children.* Cambridge, MA: Harvard University Press.

Sackney, L. E., & Dibski, D. J. (1992, August). *School-based management: A critical perspective.* Paper presented at the Seventh Regional Conference of the Commonwealth Council for Educational Administration, Hong Kong.

Sarason, S. (1990). *The predictable failure of educational reform: Can we change course before it's too late?* San Francisco: Jossey-Bass.

Schmoker, M., & Wilson, R. (1993). Transforming schools through total quality education. *Phi Delta Kappan, 74,* 389-395.

Schorr, L. (1989). *Within our reach: Breaking the cycle of disadvantage.* New York: Anchor.

Sergiovanni, T. J. (1994). *Building community in schools.* San Francisco: Jossey-Bass.

Sizer, T. (1992). *Horace's compromise: The dilemma of the American high school.* Boston: Houghton Mifflin.

Slavin, R., & Madden, N. A. (1995). Success for all: Creating schools and classrooms where all children can read. In J. Oakes & K. H. Quartz (Eds.), *Creating new educational communities: Ninety-fourth yearbook of the National Society for the Study of Education* (pp. 87-107). Chicago: University of Chicago Press.

Slavkin, M. (1995, December 31). Lift the education code dead weight. *Los Angeles Times,* p. M-5.

Smith, W. E. (1993, April). *Teachers' perceptions of role change through shared decision making: A two-year case study.* Paper presented at the annual meeting of the American Educational Research Association, Atlanta, GA.

Spady, W. (1992). *Outcome-based restructuring presentation.* Eagle, CO: The High Success Network.

Steffy, B. E. (1993). *The Kentucky education reform: Lessons for America.* Lancaster, PA: Technomic.

Stevenson, K. R., & Pellicer, L. O. (1992). School-based management in South Carolina: Balancing state-directed reform with local decision-making. In J. J. Lane & E. G. Epps (Eds.), *Restructuring schools: Problems and prospects* (pp. 123-139). Berkeley, CA: McCutchan.

Stevenson, L. (1990, September). *Local school-based management in the District of Columbia Public Schools: First impressions of pilot sites.* Washington, DC: District of Columbia Public Schools. (ERIC Document Reproduction Service No. ED 331 188)

Strusinski, M. (1991). *The continuing development of shared decision making in school-based management.* Dade County, FL: Dade County Public Schools.

Taylor, D., & Teddlie, C. (1992, April). *Restructuring and the classroom: A view from a reform district.* Paper presented at the annual meeting of the American Educational Research Association, San Francisco, CA.

Taylor, D. L., & Bogotch, I. E. (1992, January). *Teachers' decisional participation rhetoric or reality?* Paper presented at the annual meeting of the Southwest Educational Research Association, Houston, TX.

Tobias, S. (1994). Interest, prior knowledge, and learning. *Review of Educational Research, 64*(1), 37-54.

Toch, T. (1991). *In the name of excellence: The struggle to reform the nation's schools, why it's failing, and what should be done.* New York: Oxford University Press.

Tyack, D. (1993). School governance in the United States: Historical puzzles and anomalies. In J. Hannaway & M. Carnoy (Eds.), *Decentralization and school improvement* (pp. 1-32). San Francisco: Jossey-Bass.

Wagstaff, L. H., & Reyes, P. (1993). *School site-based management* (Report presented to the Educational Economic Policy Center). Austin: University of Texas, College of Education.

Watt, J. (1989). The devolution of power: The ideological meaning. *Journal of Educational Administration, 27*(1), 19-28.

Weiss, C. (1993). *Interests and ideologies in educational reform: Changing the venue of decision making in the high school* (Occasional Paper

No. 19). Cambridge, MA: National Center for Educational Leadership.

Weiss, C., & Cambone, J. (1993). *Principals' roles in shared decision making: Managing skepticism and frustration* (Occasional Paper No. 24). Cambridge, MA: National Center for Educational Leadership.

Weiss, C. H., Cambone, J., & Wyeth, A. (1991). *Trouble in paradise: Teacher conflicts in shared decision making* (Occasional Paper No. 8). Cambridge, MA: National Center for Educational Leadership.

Wildavsky, A. (1989). A cultural theory of leadership. In B. D. Jones (Ed.), *Leadership and politics: New perspectives in political science.* Lawrence: University of Kansas Press.

Wohlstetter, P., & Buffett, T. (1991, April). *School-based management in big city districts: Are dollars decentralized too?* Paper presented at the annual meeting of American Educational Research Association, Chicago.

Wohlstetter, P., & Mohrman, S. A. (1993). *School-based management: Strategies for success.* New Brunswick, NJ: CPRE Finance Briefs.

Wohlstetter, P., & Odden, A. (1992). Rethinking school-based management policy and research. *Educational Administration Quarterly, 28*(4), 529-549.

Wohlstetter, P., & Smyer, R. (1994). Models of high-performance schools. In S. A. Mohrman & P. Wohlstetter (Eds.), *School-based management: Organizing for high performance* (pp. 81-108). San Francisco: Jossey-Bass.

Index

CORWIN
PRESS

The Corwin Press logo—a raven striding across an open book—represents the happy union of courage and learning. We are a professional-level publisher of books and journals for K-12 educators, and we are committed to creating and providing resources that embody these qualities. Corwin's motto is "Success for All Learners."